Enhanced Server+ CoursePrep StudyGuide and CoursePrep ExamGuide

James Burks and Diana Buckner

COURSE TECHNOLOGY

THOMSON LEARNING ™

Australia • Canada • Mexico • Singapore • Spain • United Kingdom • United States

COURSE TECHNOLOGY

THOMSON LEARNING

Enhanced Server+ CoursePrep StudyGuide and *CoursePrep ExamGuide* by James Burks and Diana Buckner are published by Course Technology

Senior Product Manager:
Lisa Egan

Managing Editor:
Stephen Solomon

Developmental Editor:
Jill Batistick

LanWrights Product Manager:
Karen Annett

Marketing Manager:
Toby Shelton

Editorial Assistant:
Nick Lombardi

Manufacturing Manager:
Denise Sandler

Production:
Brooke Albright
Trillium Project Management

Internal Design:
GEX Publishing Services

Cover Design:
Betsy Young and Julie Malone

Composition:
GEX Publishing Services

TABLE OF CONTENTS

PREFACE

Server+ CoursePrep ExamGuide and *CoursePrep StudyGuide* are the very best tools to use to prepare for exam day. Both products provide thorough preparation for CompTIA's Server+ certification exam. CoursePrep ExamGuide and CoursePrep StudyGuide provide you ample opportunity to practice, drill, and rehearse for the exam!

COURSEPREP EXAMGUIDE

The *Server+ CoursePrep ExamGuide*, ISBN 0-619-06304-1, provides the essential information you need to master each exam objective. The ExamGuide workbook devotes an entire two-page spread to each certification objective for the Server+ exam, helping you to understand the objective, and giving you the bottom line information—what you *really* need to know. Memorize these facts and bulleted points before heading into the exam. In addition, there are seven practice-test questions for each objective on the right-hand page: that's over 600 questions total! CoursePrep ExamGuide provides the exam fundamentals and gets you up to speed quickly. If you are seeking even more opportunity to practice and prepare, we recommend that you consider our most complete solution, CoursePrep StudyGuide, which is described below.

COURSEPREP STUDYGUIDE

For those really serious about certification, we offer an even more robust solution—the *Server+ CoursePrep StudyGuide*, ISBN 0-619-06303-3. This offering includes all of the same great features you get with the CoursePrep ExamGuide workbook, including the unique two page spread, the bulleted memorization points and the practice questions. In addition, you receive a password valid for 6 months of practice on CoursePrep, a dynamic test preparation tool. The password is found in an envelope in the back cover of the CoursePrep StudyGuide. CoursePrep is a Web-based pool of hundreds of sample test questions. CoursePrep exam simulation software mimics the exact exam environment. The CoursePrep software is flexible, and allows you to practice in several ways as you master the material. Choose from Certification Mode to experience actual exam-day conditions or Study Mode to request answers and explanations to practice questions. Custom Mode lets you set the options for the practice test, including number of questions, content coverage, and ability to request answers and explanation. Follow the instructions on the inside back cover to access the exam simulation software. To see a demo of this dynamic test preparation tool, go to *www.courseprep.com*.

FEATURES

The *Server+ CoursePrep ExamGuide* and *Server+ CoursePrep StudyGuide* books include the following features:

List of domains and objectives taken directly from the CompTIA Web site The book is divided into the Server+ domains. The objectives under each domain are found within the sections. For more information about the Server+ Exam, visit CompTIA's Web site at *www.comptia.org*.

Detailed coverage of the certification objectives in a unique two-page spread Study strategically by really focusing in on the certification objectives. To enable you to do this, a two-page spread is devoted to each certification objective. The left-hand page provides the critical facts you need, while the right-hand page features practice questions relating to that objective. You'll find that the certification objective(s) and sub-objectives(s) are clearly listed in the upper left-hand corner of each spread.

An overview of the objective is provided in the ***Understanding the Objective*** section. Next, ***What You Really Need to Know*** lists bulleted, succinct facts, skills, and concepts about the objective. Memorizing these facts will be important for your success when taking the exam. ***Objectives on the Job*** places the objective in an industry perspective, and tells you how you can expect to utilize the objective on the job. This section also provides troubleshooting information.

Practice Test Questions Each right-hand page contains seven practice test questions designed to help you prepare for the exam by testing your skills, identifying your strengths and weaknesses, and demonstrating the subject matter you will face on the exam and how it will be tested. These questions are written in a similar fashion to real Server+ Exam questions. The questions test your knowledge of the objectives described on the left-hand page and also the information in the *Server+ Guide to Advanced Hardware Support* (ISBN 0-619-06202-9). You can find answers to the practice test questions on the CoursePrep Web site, *www.courseprep.com*, along with the Web-based exam preparation questions.

Glossary: Terms used in the book and other terms that you need to know for the exam are listed and defined in the glossary.

For more information: This book evolved from *Server+ Guide to Advanced Hardware Support* (ISBN 0-619-06202-9). Please refer to that book for a more in-depth explanation of concepts or procedures presented here. Course Technology publishes a full series of Server+ products, which provide thorough preparation for the Certification Exam. For more information, visit our Web site at *www.course.com/certification* or contact your sales representative.

HOW TO USE THIS BOOK

The *Server+ CoursePrep ExamGuide* and *CoursePrep StudyGuide* are all you need to successfully prepare for the Server+ Certification exam if you have some experience and working knowledge of supporting and maintaining personal computers. This book is intended to be utilized with a core text, such as *Server+ Guide to Advanced Hardware Support* (ISBN 0-619-06202-9), also published by Course Technology. If you are new to this field, use this book as a roadmap for where you need to go to prepare for certification—use the *Server+ Guide to Advanced Hardware Support* to give you the knowledge and understanding that you need to reach your goal. Course Technology publishes a full series of CompTIA products. For more information, visit our Web site at *www.course.com/certification* or contact your sales representative.

ACKNOWLEDGMENTS

We could not have completed this book without the assistance of the Course Technology staff. Your help and advice was sincerely appreciated. Thanks goes especially to Lisa Egan, Senior Product Manager, Stephen Solomon, Managing Editor, and Brooke Albright, Production Editor. In addition, we truly appreciate the assistance of Jill Batistick, Developmental Editor, for watching out for us every step of the way and helping us ensure the integrity and quality of our writing.

A special thanks also goes out to the reviewers who provided valuable input throughout the development process.

Ramona Coveny	Patrick Henry Community College
Herb Ellis	Florida Community College Jacksonville, University of North Florida
Ali Evans	Long Island University
Stephen Marchbank	Holland College

Acknowledgement from James Burks, Co-Author:

I would like to start by thanking my parents, Mary and Eddie, for everything you have given to me. To Mashone whose support and encouragement was vital to the writing of this book. To my four year old son Xavier, you are my driving force. To Jess MacPherson, George Mendez, Mark Milam, and Keith Pease for having the patience to teach and mentor. To my old friend and co-author Diana Buckner for working with me and providing valuable input on this project. To Ed, Karen, and Kim, for being the best team anyone could wish for. And last, but not least anyone who has ever taught me anything, I thank you.

From Diana Buckner, Co-Author:

First, I'd like to express my sincere gratitude and appreciation for the professional guidance, patience, and assistance I've received from Ed Tittel and Karen Annett of LANWrights, Inc. I'd also like to thank my co-author, James Burks, for being my supportive force throughout this project. I have also greatly appreciated the opportunity to work with the Course Technology staff. Lastly, I could not have completed this without my devoted parents, Bedford and Rose Buckner, who took care of my disabled son, Ziek, while I finished this project.

OBJECTIVES

1.1 Conduct pre-installation planning activities

PLAN THE INSTALLATION

UNDERSTANDING THE OBJECTIVE

The initial setup of the server and its environment is crucial. The server's stability relies on proper hardware and software configuration. By addressing a few major areas, the installation process can be completed with fewer complications and delays.

WHAT YOU REALLY NEED TO KNOW

- ◆ The role of the server may indicate its location. For example, a file server may be located in an obscure area to avoid tampering. A backup server may also be located in an area designated for access only by technical staff. On the other hand, a server configured as a domain controller may need to be in a more accessible location.

- ◆ The type of installation to be performed determines many factors. For example, a stand-alone server requires proper shelving and accessibility. Prevention of damage from external sources is crucial when installing a standalone server.

- ◆ If the server is to be rack-mounted, consult the manufacturer's documentation for installation instructions and safety precautions (for example, proper installation of the anti-tip plate and sequencing of components by weight). Plan enough space and power availability for the **keyboard, video, mouse (KVM) switch**. In addition, note the instructions for proper mounting of the cable management arm or assembly, which is used to organize cords and cables and allows for enhanced space management.

- ◆ You should consider the need for scaling and upgrades. Future enhancements may require additional space and resources. You should also consider additional storage space and cabling.

- ◆ You should consider space, power, shelving, ventilation, **local area network/wide area network (LAN/WAN)** accessibility, and temperature stability when selecting a server location.

- ◆ Secure accessibility to the server is also important. Determine in advance who will have permission to physically work with the system. The safety of the server (by using keys, locks, codes, or passes) depends on the plan to limit access to it. Document the security plan and access to the server.

- ◆ Document the entire plan completely and effectively. Make sure to note details, such as contact information for resources, original manufacturer information, and all troubleshooting steps taken, if applicable. This prevents conflicts and omissions during the installation procedure. It also provides necessary information for future engineers.

OBJECTIVES ON THE JOB

Servers are critical to businesses. Important data and access are often provided via servers, and it is critical to ensure a proper, stable installation. Planning the installation ensures that all factors have been considered. This helps minimize company costs and allows for future growth.

PRACTICE TEST QUESTIONS

1. **Which one of the following is *not* a way to obtain information about a rack installation of a server?**
   a. manufacturer's CDs
   b. installation guides/manuals
   c. Microsoft Tech Support
   d. manufacturer's support Web site

2. **Jim is responsible for the initial setup of a server to be used as a file server. A closet on the first floor is allocated for the server. What should Jim determine first?**
   a. components for backing up data
   b. proper lighting
   c. whether the server will be rack-mounted or stand-alone
   d. network cabling

3. **When mounting components into a rack, the heaviest items should be:**
   a. at the top
   b. in the middle
   c. anywhere, as long as the anti-tip plate is installed
   d. at the bottom, with the anti-tip plate installed

4. **The primary purpose for using _____ is to minimize space utilization for systems mounted in a rack.**
   a. rack fans
   b. KVM switches
   c. coaxial cabling
   d. UPSs

5. **Which of the following does *not* require consideration for planning a server installation?**
   a. disaster recovery
   b. power availability
   c. security of the server
   d. temperature of the environment

6. **Jennifer is the new network administrator for a server that was installed three years ago. Since then, no upgrades have been performed on the server's hardware. Which of the following would *not* benefit Jennifer in obtaining information on the server's initial configuration?**
   a. performance logs
   b. documentation plan of the initial installation
   c. original manufacturer documentation on all components
   d. security plan

1.1 Conduct pre-installation planning activities (continued)

VERIFY THE INSTALLATION PLAN • VERIFY HARDWARE COMPATIBILITY WITH OPERATING SYSTEM

UNDERSTANDING THE OBJECTIVE

To ensure the success of the plan for the initial installation of the server, you should verify the installation procedures. Reviewing and verifying the installation plan minimizes complications and corporate costs.

WHAT YOU REALLY NEED TO KNOW

- ◆ You should obtain all available documentation on the server itself (for example, manuals, brochures, and **CD-ROMs**).
- ◆ Make sure to obtain all available documentation on the peripherals to be installed and configured with the server, such as **Small Computer System Interface (SCSI)** controllers, **Redundant Array of Inexpensive Disks** (**RAID**) controllers, **Network Interface Cards** (**NICs**), and tape backup devices.
- ◆ In addition, you should obtain documentation for external devices, such as additional drive pods, external tape drives, hubs, and switches.
- ◆ Locate all original service tag/system or device ID numbers for future reference. (You'll need them when attempting to obtain technical support.) This should be located with the original documentation that was shipped with the server. It is also located on the server chassis.
- ◆ Locate and file all system and device warranty information.
- ◆ Locate and document resources for all devices, such as manufacturer Web sites and technical support phone numbers.
- ◆ Investigate what the impact of performing the installation of this system will be on current network performance.
- ◆ Verify power and voltage regulations and availability for the system and devices to be installed.
- ◆ Verify that the desired hardware is compatible with the desired operating system. This is one of the most important tasks to be performed in this phase.
- ◆ Locate the current Web site for the desired operating system and then locate the hardware to be installed to ensure that it has been validated for use on the **Hardware Compatibility List** (**HCL**). Use the following **Uniform Resource Locators** (**URLs**) to get started: *www.microsoft.com/hcl*, *www.developer.novell.com/solutions/yes*, and *www.linux.com/hardware*.

OBJECTIVES ON THE JOB

Servers are one of the most crucial and expensive investments a company can make. Ensuring that the installation proceeds as planned maximizes the benefit of this resource. This also allows future problems to be resolved more quickly. For example, verifying that the hardware to be implemented is approved by the desired software vendor reduces probable failures during the installation.

PRACTICE TEST QUESTIONS

1. **John is the new network administrator for a large company that is in the process of migrating from Windows NT 4.0 to Windows 2000 Server. One of the servers has a tape drive attached. What step should John take first to ensure a problem-free migration?**
   a. Review the hardware's documentation.
   b. Go to the hardware vendor's Web site.
   c. Go to the software vendor's Web site and check for the hardware validation on the HCL.
   d. Do nothing; the migration should work with no problems.

2. **During the installation of a network server, users were not able to access files needed to complete projects for the duration of the installation. Which of the following steps would have eliminated this problem?**
   a. Ensure that proper cabling was used for the installation.
   b. Verify in advance the impact the installation will have on the network.
   c. Install fault-tolerant NICs.
   d. Check in advance for proper power availability to the system.

3. **During the installation of the new server's OS, the server froze while loading a driver for the legacy SCSI controller, which was installed by the technician just prior to loading the OS. Which of the following should be the technician's next course of action?**
   a. Abort the installation, remove the SCSI controller, and check the software vendor's HCL for validation of the controller for use with the desired OS.
   b. Abort the installation, remove the SCSI controller, and call technical support for a replacement.
   c. Retry the installation with the same components and OS.
   d. Reconfigure the SCSI controller for use with the new server and retry the OS installation.

4. **Prior to the installation of a new network server, the technician scheduled for network "downtime" to allow this process to occur. What was the primary purpose for this course of action?**
   a. to allow ample time for the installation to complete
   b. to allow time for replication across the network
   c. to increase the reliability of the domain controller in the morning when users log on to the network
   d. to minimize the impact the new server installation may have on the network and its users

5. **Which of the following does _not_ require consideration when verifying a server installation?**
   a. impact on the network
   b. power availability/requirements
   c. hardware compatibility check
   d. domain names and group information

1.1   Conduct pre-installation planning activities (continued)

**VERIFY POWER SOURCES, SPACE, UPS AND NETWORK AVAILABILITY • VERIFY
THAT ALL CORRECT COMPONENTS AND CABLES HAVE BEEN DELIVERED**

UNDERSTANDING THE OBJECTIVE

Installation of an **Uninterruptible Power Supply** (**UPS**) is a very important task when initially installing a server. Doing so ensures that in the event of a power failure or lag, the server is allowed ample time for a graceful shutdown, as opposed to an unexpected shutdown that can result in file loss, corruption of data, or an inability to restart the server. Proper cabling is also very important during the initial server setup. Overall network functionality may be seriously impeded due to improper cabling.

WHAT YOU REALLY NEED TO KNOW

- ◆ UPSs vary widely in the type of power voltages they supply, the length of time for which they can provide power, and the number of devices that can be supported in the event of power loss. Obtain all available technical documentation on the UPS, including driver update information, manufacturer Web site information, and technical support resources.

- ◆ Consideration of the server's role on the network is imperative when determining what type of UPS should be used. The two categories of UPSs are standby and online.

- ◆ An online UPS uses A/C power from the wall outlet to continually charge its battery, while providing power to the server at all times. The charged battery then takes over for a specified amount of time in the event of power loss. A standby UPS charges from the wall outlet and provides voltage to the system in the event of power loss. If power is restored, the UPS then assumes a "standby" role once again.

- ◆ In Windows NT 4.0, if you don't have a serial mouse connected to a **communications (COM) port**, it may be necessary to disable the SERMOUSE driver, because NT will incorrectly detect the UPS attached to the COM port as a serial mouse.

- ◆ Cabling provides the foundation of the physical layer of the network. It is the medium that transfers the data from node to node on the network. **Coaxial**, unshielded twisted-pair, shielded twisted-pair, and **fiber optic** are the most common types of network cables. Shielded twisted-pair cables provide transmission that is less impeded by **electromagnetic interference (EMI)**.

- ◆ It is important to note where the server will be located on the network in regard to **hubs**, switches, and so on. The type of cable utilized depends on this. For example, a standard network cable should be utilized when attaching a network card to a hub.

OBJECTIVES ON THE JOB

The data and files used on a daily basis by the company are stored on the server's hard drives and tape drives. To ensure continued access to this data, a UPS must be installed to restore temporary power to the system.

PRACTICE TEST QUESTIONS

1. **Which of the following is *not* a valid cable type used with servers for network connectivity?**
   a. standard network cable with an RJ-45 connector
   b. cable using a DB-25 connector
   c. crossover cable
   d. patch cable

2. **Which of the following can cause a UPS to not be recognized by NT?**
   a. improper connectivity from UPS to wall outlet
   b. UPS not charged
   c. printer not connected to parallel port
   d. serial mouse not connected to COM port

3. **What is the role of an online UPS?**
   a. to provide enough power for the server to shut down gracefully in the event of power loss only
   b. to provide power to the server at all times
   c. to continually charge itself while providing power to the server at all times
   d. to provide power to other servers on the network in the event of power loss

4. **Prior to setting up his server, Rik noticed that there were only crossover cables available. What type of cabling connects an Ethernet network card to a hub?**
   a. serial cable with a DB-25 connector
   b. coaxial cable with a BNC connector
   c. fiber optic cable with an RS-232 interface
   d. Category 5 (8 wire) cable with an RJ-45 connector

5. **During the initial installation of a new server for her company, Susan noticed that the UPS to be configured for use with the new server was quite a bit older than the rest of the equipment being installed. She verified the UPS on the OS's HCL. What should be her next course of action?**
   a. Locate the UPS manufacturer's Web site and download the latest updates and patches for use with the new system and desired OS.
   b. Check with the server manufacturer for UPS compatibility.
   c. Order a new UPS; the old one won't work with the system/OS.
   d. Contact the UPS vendor for the latest hardware for the UPS.

6. **Carlos is the network administrator for a small firm. The company's corporate offices are located in an older building downtown, which often experiences power surges and brownouts. What is the best UPS solution available to ensure constant power to the company's server?**
   a. Purchase and install a standby UPS.
   b. Use a surge protector between the server and the wall outlet.
   c. Purchase and install an online UPS.
   d. Use a surge suppressor between the server and the wall outlet.

OBJECTIVES

1.2 Install hardware using ESD best practices

MOUNT THE RACK INSTALLATION

UNDERSTANDING THE OBJECTIVE

Servers are stored and managed in different environments. A **rack** is one of the safest and most suitable methods for a server to be installed and used. A rack is a cabinet-type chassis designed to hold servers, peripherals, and cables. Most racks have locking doors and removable panels, which provide easier access to the systems and their peripherals. Technicians must be familiar with how to rack-mount a server and how to dismount and access the server within a rack.

WHAT YOU REALLY NEED TO KNOW

- ◆ It is important to understand that a **Unit of Measure (U)** is equal to 1.75 inches. Rack dimensions, server chassis, and peripherals are commonly referred to in this manner. For example, the Cybex AutoView 400 switch supports **Universal Serial Bus (USB)** computers and Sun workstations in a 1 U chassis. In other words, the chassis for the switch is merely 1.75 inches tall.
- ◆ When planning the rack server installation, it is important to consider the units of measure for proper space allocation.
- ◆ Most manufacturers have rack installation planning guides. It is recommended to use a guide to avoid improper weight distribution, voltage irregularities, or temperature regulation problems.
- ◆ Most rack chassis are equipped with locking doors and keys. For obvious reasons, this is one of the most secure environments for a server and its peripherals.
- ◆ In general, components weighing the most are installed at the bottom of the rack first.
- ◆ Racks also come with **cable management arms (CMAs)** or assemblies that provide a less troublesome environment for cabling, which can quickly become a mess.
- ◆ Installation of an anti-tip plate is also very important. Racks can be ordered in the size of 42 U, which is approximately six feet tall. Anti-tip measures should be taken at all costs to avoid serious damage to staff and equipment.
- ◆ In most cases, a KVM switch is installed to decrease the number of peripherals needed to manage multiple servers in a rack. Using a KVM switch allows the server technician to manage multiple servers with one keyboard, video, and mouse.
- ◆ Using a KVM switch also decreases cabling. For example, if two servers are installed in the same rack, they can share the KVM switch and utilize one set of cables for each server to attach to the KVM switch only.

OBJECTIVES ON THE JOB

Rack server solutions are rapidly improving and becoming less complicated. For example, some manufacturers are now using rack installation rails that snap into place, as opposed to requiring tools, bolts, and diagrams. Understanding the benefits and processes for server rack installations greatly enhances the technician's ability to manage the server environment effectively and safely.

PRACTICE TEST QUESTIONS

1. **When referring to a 24 U rack, what does the "U" indicate?**
   a. the standard size of the rack
   b. the unit of measure, approximately 1.75 inches
   c. the number of devices the rack can hold
   d. the width of the entire rack

2. **Which of the following is usually *not* installed on a rack chassis?**
   a. fans
   b. cable management assemblies
   c. locks on doors
   d. additional serial ports

3. **Bob, the evening network administrator for a large company, wants to learn more about how to mount a server into a rack and how a rack should be utilized. Which of the following is the best source of information for Bob?**
   a. rack solutions guides provided by the rack chassis manufacturer
   b. system documentation on CDs that were shipped with the new server
   c. the software vendor's Web site for the desired OS for the server
   d. previous installation documentation left for Bob by the prior administrator

4. **Which of the following provides the most rational and adequate security for the server and its peripherals when rack-mounted?**
   a. a paid security guard to patrol the server area
   b. locks on the rack chassis doors
   c. alarm systems for the building and server room
   d. video monitoring of the server area 24 hours a day

5. **Which of the following requires the most space within the rack chassis?**
   a. a 1 U KVM switch
   b. a new 7 U server
   c. a new 2 U Web appliance
   d. a cable management assembly

6. **Kim is installing three new servers into a 42 U rack chassis. What is the simplest way she can minimize the amount of cabling necessary for these systems and their peripherals?**
   a. Install a KVM switch.
   b. Use patch cables.
   c. Install the same brands of servers.
   d. Install the same brands of monitors and keyboards.

1.2   Install hardware using ESD best practices (continued)

CUT AND CRIMP NETWORK CABLING

UNDERSTANDING THE OBJECTIVE

Network cables are the physical layer and foundation of the LAN. Category 5 is the most common type of network cable used today for 10Base-T and 100Base-TX networks. This section covers the highlights of making reliable network cables.

WHAT YOU REALLY NEED TO KNOW

- ◆ **Category 5 cable** is available in reel-in-box packaging. This packaging decreases the tangling often associated with making lengthy cables.
- ◆ To make reliable network cables, it is important to know how to use the tools required. Tools needed to make cables include the following: a **modular crimping tool**, a **universal stripping tool**, and **diagonal cutters**.
- ◆ A modular crimping tool is used to secure the wires from the Category 5 cable into the **Registered Jack-45 (RJ-45)** connector. **Crimping** is the process by which the wires from the cable are inserted into the RJ-45 connector and secured into place. Modular crimping tools have cutting and stripping capabilities; however, they often do not provide the cleanest cuts on the ends of the wires and are difficult to use when stripping the plastic covering off the wires.
- ◆ A universal stripping tool makes a neater cut and provides more control to the technician when stripping the plastic sheath off the cables and wires. Diagonal cutters enhance the technician's ability to fine-tune stripping and cutting techniques.
- ◆ There are eight wires in a Category 5 cable. They are four twisted pairs, each individually insulated. Each pair is color-coded, with one wire solid-colored (blue, orange, green, or brown) twisted around a second wire with a white background and a stripe of the same color. Half of these wires are transmitters and half are receivers. The two most common configurations of these cables are a straight-through cable (**EIA/TIA 568A**) and a crossover cable (**EIA/TIA 568B**).
- ◆ To make a straight-through cable, the wires must be untwisted and flattened on the end. Strip the wires on the end no more than one half inch. Any longer than that and this cable is more susceptible to crosstalk. Arrange the wires *on both ends of the cable* in the following order: 1-white with green stripe, 2-solid green, 3-white with orange stripe, 4-solid blue, 5-white with blue stripe, 6-solid orange, 7-white with brown stripe, and 8-solid brown.
- ◆ To make a crossover cable, arrange the wires *as above on one end and as follows on the other end*: 1-white w/brown stripe, 2-solid orange, 3-white w/green stripe, 4-solid blue, 5-white w/blue stripe, 6-solid green, 7-white w/brown stripe, and 8-solid brown.

OBJECTIVES ON THE JOB

Understanding how to create and test cables resolves many problematic issues when installing and configuring a server for networking, as does understanding cable-testing procedures.

PRACTICE TEST QUESTIONS

1. **Dave was asked to check for cabling and jacks in the room where a new server for an Ethernet network is to be installed. Which of the following information and supplies will *not* assist Dave with the installation and integration of this server?**
   a. RJ-11 connections available
   b. hub and/or switch port usage
   c. EMI levels in the room
   d. a box of Category 5 network cables with RJ-45 connectors

2. **Joan made a new set of network cables. She made a straight-through cable and tested it. When she attached the cable to the server and the network, network performance was diminished. What is one reason this may have occurred?**
   a. Joan needs to reboot the server.
   b. Crosstalk and/or noise was caused by improper stripping of the cable ends.
   c. Joan needs to reload the protocols on the server.
   d. Joan needs to create a crossover cable.

3. **What is the connector type used for standard Ethernet cables?**
   a. DB-45
   b. RJ-45
   c. 9-pin serial connector
   d. RJ-11

4. **Which of the following tools is *not* necessary for Bill to create his new set of standard Ethernet network cables?**
   a. modular crimping tool
   b. diagonal cutter
   c. universal stripping tool
   d. cable management assembly

5. **What is the physical difference between a straight-through network cable and a crossover cable?**
   a. The connectors on the ends
   b. One uses Category 3 cable and one uses Category 5 cable.
   c. Two pairs of the eight wires are switched on one end of the cable.
   d. There is no difference.

6. **How many wires are in a standard Category 5 network cable?**
   a. eight
   b. six pairs
   c. 10
   d. three pairs

1.2   Install hardware using ESD best practices (continued)

INSTALL UPS

UNDERSTANDING THE OBJECTIVE

Installation of a UPS ensures that the server has ample time for a graceful shutdown in the event of power loss or compensation for lack of power when experiencing lags or **brownouts**. For normal operation, the **Basic Input/Output System** (**BIOS**), UPS software, and the UPS itself must be configured properly.

WHAT YOU REALLY NEED TO KNOW

◆ When installing a UPS, remove the front cover, attach the battery on the inside (UPSs are shipped with the battery disconnected), and then allow the UPS to charge for the recommended amount of time prior to attaching the unit to the server.

◆ Depending on the brand of UPS, installation can be performed by attaching the serial cable from the UPS to the server and from the UPS to the wall outlet, and then booting the server. Use the driver provided by the UPS manufacturer or download the appropriate driver from the manufacturer's Web site for the appropriate **operating system** (**OS**). Verify that you are using the most up-to-date driver and patches, if needed.

◆ UPS manufacturers have appropriate software and interfaces for UPS management and usage within multiple OS platforms.

◆ UPSs use serial ports to connect to servers. This has been known to cause errors if not configured properly within the BIOS.

◆ Depending on the server, you must enter the BIOS and perform the following steps. Depending on where your UPS is connected, set the serial ports to one of the following:
Serial Port1: I/O 03f8 IRQ 4 (COM1)
Serial Port2: I/O 02f8 IRQ 3 (COM2)

◆ Often, other configurations need to be made to the software. For example, to configure the APC UPS for Windows NT, you should ensure that the **Input/Output** (**I/O**) and **Interrupt Request** (**IRQ**) port settings match those set in the BIOS. Change the COM port settings to the following: baud rate, 2400; number of data bits, 8; number of stop bits, 1; parity, none; and flow control, Xon/Xoff.

◆ It is possible to test your UPS software configuration by using HyperTerminal.

◆ To test the UPS for recovery from a power loss, simulate a power loss situation and time the UPS to determine its maximum power cycle time for the server.

OBJECTIVES ON THE JOB

UPS installation and management is a fundamental aspect of server management. Keep in mind that a UPS is another device that requires routine updates and management to ensure its proper functioning in the event that it must perform a power recovery for the server.

PRACTICE TEST QUESTIONS

1. **During the initial setup of a new server and UPS, the technician was unable to get the OS to recognize the UPS. What was the most likely cause of this problem?**
   a. The serial port was not set to the COM port for the UPS.
   b. The wrong driver was loaded.
   c. The wrong type of cable was used.
   d. The UPS voltage was set too high.

2. **Joan wants to install a new UPS. Which of the following does *not* need to be performed?**
   a. Joan needs to reboot the server.
   b. Joan should attach the battery cable inside the UPS and allow it to charge for the recommended amount of time.
   c. Joan needs to reload the protocols on the server.
   d. Joan needs to create a crossover cable.

3. **What is the connector type used for a UPS cable?**
   a. DB-45
   b. RJ-45
   c. 9-pin serial connector
   d. RJ-11

4. **Which of the following tools allows Bill to verify the UPS software's configuration?**
   a. PING
   b. HyperTerminal
   c. WINIPCFG
   d. Tracert

5. **A network administrator is preparing to teach his assistants the purpose of using a UPS. In what instances is a UPS beneficial to the server and the network?**
   a. thunderstorms
   b. in older buildings where power surges and lags occur often
   c. brownouts
   d. all of the above

6. **When Eddie received the new UPS, he plugged it in to charge for the recommended amount of time. After installing it on the server, he noticed there were still no lights on the UPS. What was the probable cause of this problem?**
   a. The UPS was defective.
   b. The UPS cable was not attached on the inside of the UPS when it was received.
   c. The UPS was not compatible with the server.
   d. Eddie used the wrong cable to attach the UPS to the server.

OBJECTIVES

1.2   Install hardware using ESD best practices (continued)

VERIFY SCSI ID CONFIGURATION AND TERMINATION

UNDERSTANDING THE OBJECTIVE

In order to install and remove components from a server, or any computer, a technician should understand the basics of SCSI. It is a standard for connecting peripherals to a computer via a standard hardware interface, which uses standard SCSI commands. The SCSI standard can be divided into SCSI (SCSI-1), SCSI-2 (SCSI Wide and SCSI Wide and Fast), and now SCSI-3. It can best be described as another type of controller for a computer that allows the transfer of signals at a much faster rate than **Integrated Drive Electronics (IDE)**.

WHAT YOU REALLY NEED TO KNOW

◆ Each SCSI device has a unique identifier (ID) from 0–7, 0–16, or 0–31, depending on the type of SCSI controller to which it is attached. The host adapter (controller itself) is usually SCSI ID 7.

◆ Remember, each SCSI device must have a unique ID. SCSI IDs can be set manually with a jumper or DIP switch on the devices, or by the controller and backplane (for hard drives).

◆ Because device IDs are determined manually or by the controller, device position on the cable is irrelevant. Any device (ID) can take any position on the bus. However, faster devices should always take the lower IDs. Having slower devices in a beginning position on the bus could slow the speed of all the devices on the chain or cause errors and malfunctions.

◆ All SCSI buses require termination. This means that each end of the cable must have a device set to terminate the bus or a piece of hardware known as a terminator. This allows the signals that are traveling up and down the bus to die down at the ends of the bus as opposed to bouncing back and forth, which creates errors for devices on the same bus. At least one end of the bus must be terminated by a device and not just another terminator.

◆ Note the following SCSI types and termination of each:

SCSI Type	Speed (MHz)	Termination
Ultra	20	passive
Ultra Wide	40	passive
Ultra 2	40	passive
Wide Ultra 2 or LVD	80	active
Ultra SCSI or SCSI-3	160	active

OBJECTIVES ON THE JOB

SCSI device management is an integral part of the server installation process. Every technician should become familiar with SCSI device IDs and termination issues. This resolves many problems in the server environment.

PRACTICE TEST QUESTIONS

1. **What SCSI ID is the host adapter usually assigned?**
    a. 7
    b. 1
    c. the lowest possible ID
    d. The host adapter does not use a SCSI ID.

2. **Which of the following is *not* a method of assigning SCSI IDs?**
    a. backplane
    d. jumpers
    c. DIP switch
    d. manually changing the SCSI ID within the OS

3. **What is the connector type used for an Ultra SCSI device?**
    a. DB-45
    b. 50-pin or 68-pin connector
    c. 9-pin serial connector
    d. RJ-11

4. **Ed wants to install a new SCSI device onto an existing SCSI chain of devices. Ultra 2 is the SCSI type of the new device. The other devices on the chain are all Ultra Wide devices. Which of the following is a valid configuration for these devices?**
    a. These devices cannot exist on the same chain.
    b. Active terminators are required on the chain due to the Fast devices.
    c. The slower devices should be on the lowest SCSI IDs.
    d. The faster devices should be on the lower SCSI IDs.

5. **What problems might a technician face when troubleshooting a SCSI ID conflict?**
    a. The CD-ROM drive may not be seen by the OS, but will have power.
    b. The tape drive will not respond to the OS, but will have power.
    c. The server will randomly shut down.
    d. all of the above

6. **Kim recently added a SCSI device to the existing SCSI chain. She added the device onto the end of the chain. When she rebooted the server, the other devices on the chain could not be seen. Which of the following might have caused this problem?**
    a. Termination was not set on the ends of the SCSI chain.
    b. Kim needs to reload the device driver.
    c. The device is not compatible with the server's hardware.
    d. Kim used the wrong cable to attach the device to the server.

1.2 Install hardware using ESD best practices (continued)

INSTALL EXTERNAL DEVICES

UNDERSTANDING THE OBJECTIVE

The installation and removal of peripheral and additional devices is common practice with server management. Upgrades, device failures, and other issues necessitate that the technician become familiar with the proper procedures for installing these devices.

WHAT YOU REALLY NEED TO KNOW

◆ Always use preventive **electrostatic discharge** (**ESD**) practices to avoid injury and damage to the equipment to be altered. Using an anti-static wrist strap in addition to standing on an anti-static mat are very good ESD management procedures.

◆ Verify that all power to any of the devices or the system itself is completely non-existent *prior* to touching anything internal to the system or device. Ensure that any residual power on the motherboard has terminated prior to reaching inside the system.

◆ Installation of a keyboard or mouse should be performed while the system is powered off to ensure BIOS recognition of the device upon **Power-on Self-Test** (**POST**). In some cases, it may be necessary to verify that the port is enabled in the system setup (CMOS) and that the resources are available for the devices.

◆ Resource allocation is the first thing to consider when thinking about adding devices to a system. IRQs can be manually set in the BIOS. SCSI IDs should also be considered when thinking about additions to the SCSI controllers.

◆ Keyboards receive power from one of the pins on their connectors.

◆ Most server OSs do not require you to load a device driver for the keyboard and mouse. Technicians should, however, become familiar with the process of loading a video/monitor driver depending on the type of monitor, video card, and OS.

◆ Installation of monitors should always be performed carefully with all power to the server disconnected.

◆ Keep in mind that monitors are very heavy, awkward, and usually very difficult to carry. Use safety precautions at all times when moving heavy equipment of this type.

◆ Computer equipment is usually shipped in anti-static packaging. It is a very good idea to keep all anti-static packaging for storage and future use.

◆ When removing components from a system, be sure to place components in anti-static bags to prevent damage to those items.

OBJECTIVES ON THE JOB

Any time a server is to be installed, moved, or modified, it almost always involves the removal and reattachment of peripheral devices. Using common precautions for ESD protects the technician as well as the equipment. Consideration of system resources should be the first consideration when planning additions to the system, whether they are internal or external.

PRACTICE TEST QUESTIONS

1. **What does the acronym ESD stand for and mean?**
    a. Enhanced System Device; a device used to upgrade a system
    b. Electronic Service Delivery; a method used for ordering equipment
    c. Electrostatic Discharge; static electricity that can damage chips and destroy system boards, although often not seen or felt by the technician
    d. Encryption Service Detection; a type of security for the system

2. **Which of the following can use a serial port?**
    a. backplane
    b. mouse
    c. DLT tape drive
    d. drive pod

3. **Kevin needs to replace the keyboard currently in use on the server. What is the best process for replacing the keyboard?**
    a. Wearing an anti-static wrist strap, unplug the keyboard while the server is on.
    b. Power down the server. Disconnect all peripherals. Then, plug in the new keyboard and reattach the rest of the devices. Reboot the server.
    c. Power down and unplug the server, and then unplug the old keyboard. Restart the server and then attach the new keyboard so that the system can recognize the keyboard after it has rebooted.
    d. Power off the server, unplug the server, and ensure that residual power has terminated. While standing on an anti-static mat and wearing an anti-static wrist strap, unplug the keyboard currently in use. Plug in the new keyboard. Reboot the server.

4. **How does a keyboard get power?**
    a. One of the pins on the keyboard connector carries a 5-volt charge.
    b. from a battery
    c. The keyboard does not require power.
    d. from the UPS

5. **Susannah is planning to add an external tape drive to the new server. Which of the following should be considered when planning the installation of the tape drive?**
    a. the SCSI ID of the tape drive
    b. ESD preventive measures when performing the installation
    c. the power requirements of the new device
    d. all of the above

6. **Where would a technician need to ensure that a port is enabled for a new keyboard or mouse?**
    a. BIOS (system setup)
    b. within the SCSI controller's BIOS
    c. within the OS's device manager
    d. by using a DIP switch on the device itself

1.2 Install hardware using ESD best practices (continued)

VERIFY POWER-ON VIA POWER-ON SEQUENCE

UNDERSTANDING THE OBJECTIVE

The POST process allows the **central processing unit (CPU)** to verify that all attached controllers, peripherals, and devices are communicating with the processor. During this process, the system is powering up to a functional state. Learning how to identify device sounds and alerts as they power up is a very common practice in systems hardware management. The purpose of this section is to highlight the areas to be aware of during server POST sequences.

WHAT YOU REALLY NEED TO KNOW

◆ The POST process is performed by the BIOS.

◆ Errors occurring during POST before video is available are communicated in a series of beeps. This is referred to as beep codes. Information on specific beep codes is usually available on the system manufacturer's Web site.

◆ Error codes and problems with hardware devices and components are displayed on the screen after video becomes available.

◆ Error codes can be messages on the screen about a particular device or controller, or they can be numeric POST codes that are displayed.

◆ Note that components and controllers attached to the system appear in the order in which the CPU recognizes each device. If a device has been installed, but is not showing up during POST, the installation process should be verified.

◆ Note that the absence of a device during POST may also indicate a problem. For example, a server with two SCSI controllers may show only one during POST. After making sure that the controller has been enabled in the system's BIOS, this controller should display a message during the boot sequence to indicate it is recognized by the CPU.

◆ Devices that have their own power have indicator lights that power on during POST.

◆ Some controllers, such as RAID controllers, have their own alerts. For instance, when a hard drive has failed, one well-known RAID card executes an alarm. This should not be confused with the system's POST sequence.

◆ Devices are tested and matched with their device drivers during POST.

◆ Resource allocation occurs for each device during POST.

◆ After the POST process has completed, the BIOS searches for an operating system on the drives in the order in which they are listed in the system setup program.

OBJECTIVES ON THE JOB

The boot process, or POST sequence, is a very informative tool if technicians learn how to recognize errors, beep codes, and messages. Examining the system hardware and how it responds during POST provides the technician with a good baseline of knowledge. Troubleshooting is less cumbersome for the server technician who understands how each peripheral performs under normal conditions.

PRACTICE TEST QUESTIONS

1. **Henry has been teaching his new network administrator about what to look for during POST. Which of the following does *not* apply?**
   a. beep codes
   b. POST number codes
   c. error messages on display
   d. bottlenecks

2. **Upon the initial POST of a brand new, out-of-the-box server, a very long beep occurs followed by a series of short beeps. Nothing is displayed on the screen. What is the most likely cause of the beeps?**
   a. A device that should load before the video adapter has failed.
   b. The keyboard is stuck.
   c. A hard drive has failed.
   d. This is normal activity; simply reboot.

3. **Which of the following is *not* a part of the POST sequence?**
   a. The system's CPU verifies all devices and drivers.
   b. All alerts for the system are reset.
   c. The BIOS searches for an operating system.
   d. The BIOS allocates resources such as memory.

4. **Jim needs to research a particular beep code. Where can he locate this information?**
   a. the system manufacturer's Web site
   b. the software vendor's Web site for the OS
   c. the event log
   d. the system log

5. **Which of the following skills helps a server technician to evaluate the POST sequence of a new server?**
   a. listening for beep codes
   b. watching the monitor for messages
   c. watching the peripherals attached to the system for power indication lights to turn on as each device is recognized
   d. all of the above

6. **What does the term POST mean?**
   a. the sequencing of diagnostics for the CPU
   b. the verification of devices and drivers by the BIOS, including resource allocation and alerts about any errors detected
   c. the verification of the hard disk drive integrity
   d. the verification of power for the main power supply only

OBJECTIVES

2.1 Check/upgrade BIOS/firmware levels

CHECK/UPGRADE BIOS/FIRMWARE LEVELS

UNDERSTANDING THE OBJECTIVE

The BIOS contains code that defines how the system functions. The code is written to a flash memory chip that can be updated by software instead of having to be replaced. Without the BIOS, the server is unable to boot. A server technician must be able to check the BIOS revision level and upgrade the BIOS when necessary.

WHAT YOU REALLY NEED TO KNOW

◆ *Checking the BIOS Revision Level*

The BIOS revision level can be checked when the server POSTs or by using the **System Setup Utility (SSU)**. Entering the SSU is accomplished by pressing a specific key or key combination on your keyboard. This information can be obtained from your system documentation or your server vendor's Web site.

Once inside the utility, you will see settings for the different devices in the system. Some of the settings are for information only, whereas other settings allow you to make changes to their configuration. Never change a setting in the utility unless it is a necessary change. Doing so could cause the server not to boot.

◆ *Upgrading the BIOS Revision Level*

Before attempting to perform a BIOS upgrade, verify that the upgrade is compatible with your server's hardware and software. Record all settings in the SSU to ensure that you are able to return the setup to its original settings.

The BIOS update is located at the server vendor's Web site. The file is normally an executable file that creates the actual disks for the upgrade. The program makes the first disk bootable and copies the data to the disk(s). Boot the server to the diskette and follow the directions to complete the update. Never power off or reset the server during a flash (or upgrade); doing so could render the motherboard inoperable and require a replacement.

After the upgrade has completed, verify that it installed successfully by entering the SSU and checking the revision level. In addition, you should verify that devices in the utility are configured properly. Then, save any changes made to the SSU, remove all diskettes, and boot the server.

Document any changes made to the system for future reference.

OBJECTIVES ON THE JOB

The BIOS makes all system activities possible. Vendors are constantly finding ways to improve the way hardware and software interact. A technician should be aware of the BIOS functions and all settings in the SSU. When a BIOS upgrade is available, a technician must verify that the BIOS is completely compatible with hardware and software prior to upgrading.

PRACTICE TEST QUESTIONS

1. **Russell has been given the task of upgrading the BIOS on a Windows 2000 server running a database application. The server has two network cards and a RAID controller. Which of the following items should be checked for BIOS compatibility? (Choose all that apply.)**
   - a. database application
   - b. RAID controller
   - c. network cards
   - d. operating system

2. **Charles just updated the BIOS on his department's Windows 2000 server. He notices that during POST, the server is loading the embedded devices before loading his RAID controller. This causes the system not to boot. What could possibly cause this problem?**
   - a. The BIOS update changed the settings in the SSU.
   - b. The firmware for all embedded devices did not update.
   - c. The flash did not update successfully.
   - d. The BIOS flash is corrupt.

3. **The BIOS revision level can be verified when a server boots by: (Choose all that apply.)**
   - a. verifying the information displayed at POST
   - b. booting the server with a bootable DOS diskette
   - c. pressing a key or combination of keys and entering the BIOS
   - d. changing the jumper settings on the motherboard

4. **Sam downloaded the BIOS from the server vendor's Web site. When Sam tries to flash the BIOS, he receives a message that his BIOS is newer than the one he is trying to flash and the flash terminates. What could possibly cause the error?**
   - a. The installation disk(s) is (are) corrupt.
   - b. The settings on the motherboard need to be cleared by setting jumpers.
   - c. Sam downloaded the wrong file for the upgrade.
   - d. Sam has a bad motherboard.

5. **Franklin has just updated the BIOS on 10 NetWare 4.11 servers. Which step or steps should he perform next to complete his task?**
   - a. Verify that the BIOS updated successfully.
   - b. Document all changes and the new revision for future reference.
   - c. Enter the SSU and verify that all settings are correct.
   - d. all of the above

6. **Leigh has been given the task of upgrading the BIOS on all servers in his organization. All of the servers are from the same manufacturer. There are two identical department servers, a department class server, and two enterprise class servers. How many files must Leigh download to complete this task?**
   - a. 2
   - b. 3
   - c. 4
   - d. 5

2.1   Check/upgrade BIOS/firmware levels (continued)

CHECK/UPGRADE BIOS/FIRMWARE LEVELS (CONTINUED)

UNDERSTANDING THE OBJECTIVE

The firmware of a device (hard drive, RAID controller, tape backup unit, and so on) is vital to the functionality of the device. Firmware is device-specific software that has been written to a chip that is embedded on the device. The firmware can be updated by running a firmware update utility provided by the hardware vendor or manufacturer. As a server technician, you must know how to determine the firmware revision for a device and update the firmware when necessary.

WHAT YOU REALLY NEED TO KNOW

◆ *Checking the Firmware*

Verifying the **firmware** varies depending on the device. With some devices, such as RAID controllers and SCSI controllers, the firmware revision level is displayed at POST. In other devices, such as tape backup units, you verify the firmware inside the OS or by running specific diagnostic utilities for the device.

◆ *Upgrading the Firmware*

Before attempting to perform a firmware upgrade, verify compatibility with your server's hardware and software. Firmware updates can be downloaded from the hardware vendor's Web site. The file is normally an executable file that creates the necessary disk(s) for the upgrade. After the disks have been created, you have to obtain or create a bootable diskette. You should boot the server with the boot disk and execute the program on the firmware disks after the server has booted.

Never shut down or restart a server during a firmware update; doing so could cause the device being updated to fail, resulting in the need to replace the device. After the update has completed, remove the disks and reboot the server. You can verify that the firmware level updated successfully by checking the firmware. As always, document any changes made to the system for future reference.

OBJECTIVES ON THE JOB

After troubleshooting a device, you will discover that in some instances the only way to fix specific problems is to upgrade the firmware for the device. Tape backup units, RAID controllers, and SCSI controllers all have firmware. As a technician, you must know your hardware and its firmware levels. Vendors are constantly updating the firmware for devices, and you should ensure that you have the latest firmware revision for your specific server platform.

PRACTICE TEST QUESTIONS

1. **Paul is performing a firmware upgrade for the tape backup unit installed in his server. Although the server LEDs are showing activity, the server is responding slowly. What should Paul do?**
   - a. Press the Restart button on the server and restart the upgrade.
   - b. Press Escape to halt the upgrade and restart the upgrade.
   - c. Let the upgrade continue until it completes.
   - d. Power off the server, reboot, and restart the upgrade.

2. **Todd has been given the task of obtaining the firmware level for all the tape backup units in the server room. All the servers are running NT 4.0 Service Pack 4. How can Todd verify the firmware revision of the tape backup units without shutting down the server?**
   - a. Verify the firmware revision under tape devices in the Control Panel.
   - b. Run uptomp.exe at the c:\ prompt.
   - c. Edit the tapeinfo.dat file located in the Winnt/System32 folder.
   - d. Display properties for the device using Task Manager.

3. **Upgrading the firmware for a device requires you to obtain the latest revision for the device. Who would most likely have the firmware revision required? (Choose all that apply.)**
   - a. OS CDs
   - b. the server vendor's Web site
   - c. the hardware vendor's Web site
   - d. the third-party software vendor

4. **Tim was updating the firmware for his RAID controller when a power outage occurred in the building. After power was returned to normal, Tim tried to restart the upgrade but received errors during the process. When Tim tried to boot the server, the server did not boot. What could possibly be the cause of this problem? (Choose all that apply.)**
   - a. The RAID select jumper needs to be set on the motherboard.
   - b. The RAID controller was damaged during the power outage and needs to be replaced.
   - c. The firmware was never updated, but was damaged due to the power outage.
   - d. The server BIOS is corrupt.

5. **Which of the following devices would *not* have a firmware revision?**
   - a. tape backup unit
   - b. network card
   - c. power supply
   - d. RAID controller

6. **Ted created two disks required to upgrade the firmware for his RAID controller. When Ted attempted to boot from the disks, he received a "Missing Operating System" message. What is the most likely cause?**
   - a. The first disk is bad.
   - b. Ted needs a bootable disk.
   - c. Ted downloaded the wrong firmware.
   - d. The floppy drive is bad.

2.2 Configure RAID

CONFIGURE RAID

UNDERSTANDING THE OBJECTIVE

Fault tolerance and redundancy are the purpose behind RAID. With hardware RAID, hard disk drives are configured in specific arrays to optimize a fault-tolerant or redundant server environment. Depending on the configuration chosen and the RAID controller's capabilities, the RAID controller itself can even be programmed to use a hot spare, or an alternate hard drive, to recover from a disk failure. Software RAID is also a form of redundancy. It is not a form of fault tolerance, however, because the data is still all physically located on the same disk.

WHAT YOU REALLY NEED TO KNOW

- ◆ **Fault tolerance** is the capacity for a system to continue to perform despite unexpected hardware or software malfunctions.
- ◆ **Redundancy** is a technique in which components or machines are used in duplicate on the network. For example, one entire server may have an exact duplicate in the event that the original system fails.
- ◆ Although there are multiple physical drives in one RAID array, the computer sees them as one logical drive or storage unit. For example, a RAID controller may have three 4 GB hard drives in an array, but address the storage capacity wholly as 12 GB.
- ◆ A major benefit to utilizing a RAID array is speed. Data can be written to or read from the disks at incredible speeds. It is important to note that the different levels of RAID provide varying speeds for read and write performance. For instance, RAID level 1 is known as disk mirroring. With this configuration, hard drives are paired. One hard drive is the original, functioning drive. The second is an exact duplicate of the first and is always ready in the event that the first drive fails. Data is written to the second drive concurrently as the data is written to the first drive. This process takes longer than just writing data to one drive; however, this is a very reliable RAID configuration.
- ◆ There are varying levels of RAID. The most common levels are 0, 1, 5, and 10. The next section covers the configuration of these levels.
- ◆ In the event of hard disk drive failure with a software RAID configuration, data has not been duplicated onto another physical drive; therefore, data is likely compromised.

OBJECTIVES ON THE JOB

The major goal of every server technician should be to optimize the server and its environment, to limit downtime, and to decrease costly emergency repairs that can occur when components of a server experience hardware or software malfunctions. One effective method of addressing all of these issues is to verify that data is being stored in an array. There are many options for the configuration of an array; a server technician should become very familiar with the installation, configuration, and rebuilding and repairing processes of these highly data-sensitive server configurations.

PRACTICE TEST QUESTIONS

1. **What are the two main purposes of RAID?**
    a. hot swapping and cost
    b. fault tolerance and redundancy
    c. security and cost
    d. redundancy and security

2. **What are two forms of RAID?**
    a. software and logical
    b. hardware and logical
    c. physical and logical
    d. hardware and software

3. **While attempting to configure the new RAID array after installing three 2 GB hard disk drives, Robert noticed that the OS recognized only one large drive. What was the reason for this?**
    a. Although there are multiple physical drives, they are recognized as one logical drive until configured differently.
    b. The OS did not correctly recognize two of the three hard disk drives.
    c. The OS needs to be updated with the latest patches.
    d. Robert did not reboot the system.

4. **Susan noticed a hardware failure indication alert on the system configured as a server for her company's small network. She had one hard disk drive and had configured it with a software RAID solution. If the hard drive has failed, which of the following statements is the most likely outcome?**
    a. Susan cannot access her data without going into the RAID controller's BIOS and reformatting the drive.
    b. Susan's data is not truly fault tolerant; therefore, it may be corrupted or completely inaccessible.
    c. Susan's data is fine because the software RAID solution is completely fault tolerant.
    d. She must move the pin on the hard drive's jumper block to RAID 2 to recover her data.

5. **Bob is the accounting manager. He has asked for a storage solution that guarantees recovery of all data in the event of hardware/software malfunctions with as little recovery time as possible. The server technician recommended a RAID level 1. Which of the following will *not* be a benefit of using RAID 1 in this situation?**
    a. decreased downtime and less expensive repair costs in the event of hardware failures
    b. the speed of read/write access due to the double access to hard drives
    c. true fault tolerance/redundancy
    d. all of the above

2.2   Configure RAID (continued)

CONFIGURE RAID

UNDERSTANDING THE OBJECTIVE

Configuration of the various RAID levels varies somewhat depending on the controller used. The major RAID levels used today are 0, 1, 5, and 10. A fundamental concept to understanding the various RAID levels is striping. In this section, we review the common RAID levels used today.

WHAT YOU REALLY NEED TO KNOW

◆ **Striping** is a method of concatenating multiple drives into one logical storage unit by partitioning each drive's storage space into stripes, which may be as small as one sector (512 bytes) or as large as several megabytes. The stripes are then written to the drive in a round-robin fashion so that the combined space is compiled alternately of stripes from each drive.

◆ In RAID 0 (striping), data is split across drives, resulting in higher data throughput. Because no redundant information is stored, performance is very good, but the failure of any disk in the array results in data loss. Only one drive is required to configure this level of RAID. This is the fastest and most efficient array type, but offers no fault tolerance. This can be configured by selecting the hard drive(s) from within the controller's BIOS and setting the desired drives to RAID 0.

◆ RAID 1 (mirroring) provides redundancy by writing all data to two or more drives. The performance of a RAID 1 array tends to be faster on reads and slower on writes as compared to a single drive, but if either drive fails, no data is lost. This can be configured by selecting the pairs of drives to be mirrored from within the controller's BIOS and specifying RAID 1.

◆ RAID 5 (striping with parity) distributes parity among the drives. At least three drives are required for RAID 5 arrays. Note that with this level, one drive can fail in the array, because the remaining drives will use the parity bits to function. If an additional drive fails, however, data is lost. This can be configured from within the controller's BIOS by selecting the drives (at least three) and specifying RAID 5.

◆ RAID 10 (RAID 1 and RAID 0 combined) is implemented as a striped array whose segments are RAID 1 arrays; it has the same fault tolerance as RAID 1, and it has the same overhead for fault tolerance as mirroring alone. Additionally, high I/O rates are achieved by striping RAID 1 segments and, under certain circumstances, a RAID 10 array can sustain multiple simultaneous drive failures. It is important to remember that regardless of the number of physical drives in one RAID array, the computer sees them all as one logical drive or storage unit. After creating the desired array, the user then configures the space for partitioning.

OBJECTIVES ON THE JOB

The preservation of sound data is the goal of RAID implementation. Every server technician should be comfortable with the implementation of each level and its benefits.

PRACTICE TEST QUESTIONS

1. _____ distributes parity among the drives.
   a. Hot-swap implementation
   b. RAID 5
   c. RAID 1
   d. RAID 0

2. Highly critical data is stored on a server with five hard drives. Data integrity is the main concern. Currently, the drives are not set up in an array. What would be the best RAID level for this scenario?
   a. software RAID
   b. RAID 5
   c. RAID 0
   d. RAID 1

3. _____ is a method of combining hard drives into an array and configuring a controller to distribute data bits to each in a specific manner.
   a. A software RAID
   b. A Linux RAID
   c. Implementing a hardware RAID
   d. A hot-spare implementation

4. Susan noticed a hard drive failure alert on the system configured as a server for her company's small network. The two hard drives are configured in a RAID 1 array. What will happen to the data if one of the drives has failed?
   a. The data will be lost because there was no redundancy.
   b. The data will be recoverable because she had a current backup.
   c. The data will be corrupted because it has only portions of the data from the original drive.
   d. The data will be fine because the two drives are mirrored and the remaining drive is an exact duplicate of the failed drive.

5. What is the minimum number of drives required to configure a RAID 0 array?
   a. three
   b. one
   c. two
   d. four

6. What is the minimum number of drives required to configure a RAID 10 array?
   a. three
   b. one
   c. four
   d. two

2.3 Install NOS

INSTALL NOS

UNDERSTANDING THE OBJECTIVE

The software portion of the server configuration is often the most challenging because many driver conflicts and firmware issues arise during this phase. A server technician should have already performed the installation planning and the hardware verification, and obtained all drivers, patches, and service packs that may be needed to complete the installation of the desired OS. This section highlights best practices to ensure a stable network OS installation.

WHAT YOU REALLY NEED TO KNOW

- ◆ Each individual OS has basic requirements. Ensure that the server has the resources needed for the OS to function at its best.
- ◆ It is good practice to perform a clean installation—instead of an upgrade—on a server to ensure that there is no corruption of data. A low-level format is a recommended beginning to a clean installation.
- ◆ Each server manufacturer's Web site should be checked for the desired OS's installation guides because the manufacturer often has documented steps necessary to load devices and drivers; reading these guides might eliminate many hours of troubleshooting on the technician's part.
- ◆ Server manufacturers have developed another method of installing an OS on a server that prevents many hours of searching for drivers, patches, and updates: the bootable **compact disc** (**CD**). This CD provides the user with options for the installation, and it loads the OS, drivers, and utilities that are often necessary to perform upgrades and integrity checks throughout the life of the server.
- ◆ How you install the OS (using a bootable CD or floppies or performing an installation across the network) determines what you need to perform your installation. The OS version and the server manufacturer are also important considerations during the installation process. For example, one server manufacturer has a bootable floppy, which enables the functionality of virtually any CD-ROM drive by providing the appropriate drivers. It is then possible to proceed with the CD-ROM installation of your OS. This utility is free and may be downloaded from the manufacturer's Web site.
- ◆ For OS installation from a bootable CD-ROM to occur, it may also be necessary to enter the system's setup utility to set the boot sequence to CD first, as systems often are set to boot from floppy drives or hard drives.
- ◆ Another consideration for the installation is the size of the partition on which you are installing the OS. Again, there are minimal requirements for each OS and you must follow those recommendations to ensure a stable OS.

OBJECTIVES ON THE JOB

The OS integrity is the responsibility of the server technician. By following the steps previously noted, the technician will create a stable OS.

PRACTICE TEST QUESTIONS

1. **John performed a new OS installation on a server using boot disks and an OS installation CD. After the first installation, the server hung on the OS logon. John assumed there was a problem with the installation. He performed a low-level format on the drive, using the same boot disks and CD, and then reloaded the OS. The same problem occurred. What might have caused the corruption?**
   a. hard drive corruption
   b. boot disks
   c. partitioning errors
   d. hard drive failure

2. **Which of the following will most likely cause problems when loading devices during an OS installation?**
   a. device drivers
   b. patches
   c. service packs
   d. OS version variations

3. **Which of the following should be considered prior to performing an OS installation on a server?**
   a. RAID level
   b. the number of NICs to be installed
   c. minimum requirements for the OS as indicated by the software vendor
   d. resource allocation

4. **Brian was performing an installation of NetWare 5.1 on a server. He is not familiar with the OS requirements. Where can he obtain this information?**
   a. Novell's Web site
   b. the server manufacturer's Web site
   c. the help files on the NetWare installation CDs
   d. all of the above

5. **While attempting to load an OS via CD onto the server, Cindy noted that the server would not boot to the CD. The CD is a bootable CD. Which of the following possibilities could be the solution to this problem?**
   a. She can buy another CD to replace the current one, which is likely defective.
   b. She can enter the system setup to change the boot sequence to CD first.
   c. She can use boot floppies.
   d. She can buy another CD-ROM driver to replace the current one, which is likely defective.

6. **Which of the following can cause corruption during an OS installation?**
   a. boot disks
   b. drivers downloaded from Web sites
   c. floppies used to download drivers and patches from Web sites
   d. all of the above

2.3   Install NOS (continued)

CONFIGURE NETWORK AND VERIFY NETWORK CONNECTIVITY

UNDERSTANDING THE OBJECTIVE

After a server is set up with the desired hardware configurations and the OS has been installed, configuring and verifying network connectivity is the next phase of the server technician's tasks.

WHAT YOU REALLY NEED TO KNOW

- ◆ You should consider what the role of the server is. For example, if the server is to be configured as a gateway, as opposed to a file server, specifications vary greatly with regards to protocols and services.
- ◆ You also should know which protocols need to be installed and configured. The OS and the role of the server determine which protocols you need to install and configure.
- ◆ For proper network configuration, speed settings of the devices attached to this network are important to consider. A 100-BaseT Ethernet network requires that all devices on the network be set to the same speed.
- ◆ It is important to know the transmission speed for the network. Is it full or half duplex? If set to auto-sense on some devices and specified on others, this may cause connectivity problems.
- ◆ Tools are available at multiple levels to check for network connectivity. For example, within the system setup, many servers have a loopback diagnostic test that can be performed on the NIC.
- ◆ At the **Microsoft Disk Operating System** (**MS DOS**) level, there are many tools available to gather information about network specifications. The **Packet Internet Groper** (**PING**) utility tests the network adapter itself and provides feedback on sending and receiving packets across the network. PING also is used from within other OSs to perform this function.
- ◆ **TRACERT** (or TRACEROUTE on UNIX systems) is another very common utility used to gather network information. It traces the path of a packet from the originating host to the destination host. It reports the number of router hops and packet traverses, the router's addresses, and how long the packet took to go from one place to the next.
- ◆ **NBSTAT** is a utility that reveals the **NetBIOS** names and status of connected devices running NetBIOS over **Transmission Control Protocol/Internet Protocol** (**TCP/IP**). **NETSTAT** is a similar utility that provides information about all connected TCP/IP hosts, port numbers, and status.
- ◆ Most network adapters provide a self-diagnostic test that verifies network connectivity.

OBJECTIVES ON THE JOB

Proper network configuration is a regular task for the server technician. By understanding the previously stated principles, the technician is better equipped to perform the tasks. Doing so enhances network functionality and stability, decreases network downtime, and ultimately increases productivity for the company.

PRACTICE TEST QUESTIONS

1. **While setting up a network server, Robin noted that the server would be used as a backup domain controller. Which of the following statements is true regarding the setup of this server?**
   a. The role of the server does not matter when configuring network specifications.
   b. Knowing the role of the server helps to determine specific protocols and services Robin needs to configure.
   c. A backup domain controller will not require specific network configurations.
   d. The network specifications for the backup domain controller occur automatically via the primary domain controller.

2. **Chris is the UNIX administrator for a network server. He has received multiple reports from users in one location regarding slow transfer rates. Which utility should Chris use to report on the path of the packet transfers?**
   a. NBSTAT
   b. PING
   c. TRACEROUTE
   d. PING/trace

3. **Prior to setting up a new network server, which of the following pieces of information should be gathered?**
   a. role of the server, protocols and services needed, and transmission speed on the network
   b. IP address of the server
   c. administrator password
   d. all of the above

4. **Which of the following network verification utilities is available with multiple OSs?**
   a. NBSTAT
   b. WINIPCONFIG
   c. PING
   d. all of the above

5. **When testing the loopback address utilizing the PING utility, what IP address should you PING?**
   a. Any IP address
   b. 255.255.255.0
   c. 127.0.0.0
   d. 127.0.0.1

6. **Which protocol must be installed for Internet access?**
   a. NetBEUI
   b. TCP/IP
   c. IPX/SPX
   d. all of the above

2.4 Configure external peripherals

CONFIGURE EXTERNAL PERIPHERALS

UNDERSTANDING THE OBJECTIVE

Depending on the peripherals and devices attached to the server, this portion of the server installation varies greatly. For these devices to function at an optimum state in conjunction with the server, configuration for each device may be necessary. This section highlights some of the specifications as they apply in the server environment.

WHAT YOU REALLY NEED TO KNOW

- ◆ UPS configuration options should be made as indicated in Objective 1.2 on UPS installation. Important items to consider are the recognition of the UPS by the system by configuring the appropriate serial port for the UPS and making the appropriate port specifications from within the OS. You should refer to the specific UPS manufacturer's documentation for instructions.

- ◆ In most cases, you can configure external drive pods from within the OS. If you are unable to do so, the most common method is by accessing the drives via the controller's BIOS during POST. To do so, simply press Control + A or whichever key combination is recommended when the screen prompt appears.

- ◆ External tape drives are configured from within the OS. Resource allocation for the tape drive is part of the installation process. You can configure desired tape drive functionality from within the software used to perform backups.

- ◆ KVM switches are configured in correlation with the attached devices. Remember, if you have four servers attached, you must have four sets of cables.

- ◆ **Power Distribution Units (PDUs)** are much like power strips. These should be physically configured for convenient access by all devices in the rack or server area.

- ◆ CMAs should be installed according to the manufacturer's specifications to ensure the maximum usability of the device.

- ◆ A rack fan is an external device that provides additional cooling to the servers enclosed in the rack environment. No configuration is necessary for these devices.

OBJECTIVES ON THE JOB

After the necessary configuration changes and specifications are made, the server should be ready for software optimization. Performing these steps ensures that the server is the most stable and reliable it can be for your users. The server technician's skills are greatly enhanced by understanding and performing the steps necessary to configure each peripheral device. Researching the manufacturer's Web sites for information on how to perform this effectively is also an option. Each specific manufacturer has already performed the testing and research needed to understand how to best configure a specific device to ensure it provides the maximum benefit in your server's environment.

PRACTICE TEST QUESTIONS

1. **What is the name of a device usually installed in a rack that eliminates the need for a keyboard, mouse, and monitor for each system in the rack?**
   a. BDC
   b. PDU
   c. KVM
   d. KVU

2. **Which of the following is *not* an external device for a server environment?**
   a. PDU
   b. CMOS battery
   c. UPS
   d. KVM

3. **Tony is configuring a KVM switch in a rack with five servers. How many cables does he need in order to attach the servers to the KVM switch?**
   a. 1
   b. 10
   c. 5
   d. 3

4. **While moving a rack, Rik noticed that the temperature in the rack seemed warm. The rack was purchased with optional rack fans, but they have not been installed yet. Which of the following would be a sensible solution for this problem?**
   a. Install the rack fans.
   b. Install additional fans/heat sinks on the servers.
   c. Move the rack to a cooler room.
   d. Remove one of the servers from the rack.

5. **A CMA is a device that _____.**
   a. requires configuration from within the SSU
   b. should be installed manually to manage cables and cords from the servers in the rack
   c. decreases the amount of cabling necessary for multiple servers in a rack
   d. you can manage from within the device's BIOS or from some OSs' utilities

6. **How would the configuration of an external DLT tape drive need to be performed?**
   a. by entering the system setup
   b. by using a utility within the OS or the backup software
   c. by pressing a special key combination when the tape drive appears on POST
   d. all of the above

2.5   Install NOS updates to design specifications

INSTALL NOS UPDATES TO DESIGN SPECIFICATIONS

UNDERSTANDING THE OBJECTIVE

Part of ensuring a stable OS and problem-free cooperation with all peripherals attached to the server involves "tweaking" the OS to its optimum state. In order to achieve this, the server technician is required to research the software vendor's Web site(s) for updates and patches, which may prevent known problematic issues and enhance the performance of the server and its hardware as a whole. This section highlights those issues.

WHAT YOU REALLY NEED TO KNOW

- ◆ Microsoft issues service packs for its OSs to update drivers, correct known problematic issues, and enhance performance.
- ◆ This is the current link on Microsoft's site to download service packs and releases: *http://support.microsoft.com/highlights/default.asp?pr=topsdn&cl=135&fr=0&sd=tech.*
- ◆ Novell also issues patches for these reasons. By searching the following link, the appropriate patches and updates may be downloaded for a NetWare server: *http://support.novell.com/filefinder/.*
- ◆ UNIX also issues patches and supplements for these reasons. They are available at: *http://www.sco.com/support/ftplists/index.html.*
- ◆ IBM OS/2 fixes and fixpaks can be accessed via this link: *http://www-4.ibm.com/software/os/warp/support/#Supportdownloads.*
- ◆ Not having the most current drivers and service packs applied on a server can cause many different types of problems.
- ◆ Often, when a driver is updated on a system, the service pack needs to be reapplied. This also applies when a new device driver is added to an up-and-running server system.
- ◆ Reapplying the service pack or patches may also be necessary when certain applications are loaded onto the server.
- ◆ Updates should be performed when the server can be rebooted without affecting the network and users. Not all updates require a reboot; however, it is common practice to allow ample time for unexpected problems to arise.
- ◆ Make sure to have a current backup, boot disks, **emergency repair disks** (**ERDs**), and the original OS disks on hand in the event these items become necessary.

OBJECTIVES ON THE JOB

Although the OS of choice is extremely individualized, maintaining current device drivers, updates, patches, supplements, and service packs is based on the same principles. Updates and changes of this nature can result in damage to current settings and specifications.

PRACTICE TEST QUESTIONS

1. **Becky will be installing a new RAID controller in the server that currently has Novell NetWare 5.1 installed. How should Becky prepare the server's OS for this?**
   a. Search Novell's support site for NetWare 5.1 and RAID controller compatibility issues.
   b. Perform a full system backup.
   c. Plan server downtime for the update.
   d. all of the above

2. **To which OS does the term "fixpak" apply?**
   a. UNIX
   b. Linux
   c. NetWare 5.0
   d. IBM OS/2

3. **When updating a driver or application within a Microsoft OS, which of the following should a server technician have prepared in advance?**
   a. original OS installation disk(s)
   b. ERD
   c. extra floppies
   d. none of the above

4. **David installed the latest drivers for the 3Com network adapter cards on an NT server. What should be his next course of action?**
   a. Perform a full system backup.
   b. Reapply the recommended service pack.
   c. Reload the OS.
   d. Configure network protocols.

5. **When the new NT administrator was required to perform an update on a NetWare server, he was unfamiliar with the terminology on Novell's support site for updates. What is the term Novell uses for the latest updates for their OS?**
   a. fixpaks
   b. supplements
   c. patches
   d. service updates

6. **Bob was planning to load the most current service pack on a Windows 2000 server. Which of the following is *not* necessary in the planning of this project?**
   a. Perform a full system backup.
   b. Create a driver disk for the system.
   c. Schedule server downtime.
   d. Create an emergency repair disk.

O B J E C T I V E S

2.6   Update manufacturer specific drivers

UPDATE MANUFACTURER SPECIFIC DRIVERS

UNDERSTANDING THE OBJECTIVE

After the OS and the hardware have both been configured and set to their optimum states, the server is ready to go. Another task that becomes a regular part of maintaining the server is regularly updating the device drivers on the system.

WHAT YOU REALLY NEED TO KNOW

◆ Listed below are some major manufacturers' Web sites to visit when researching the latest device driver releases. Keep in mind that just as drivers are constantly being updated, so are the manufacturers' Web sites.

◆ It is often necessary to search for device drivers at specific vendor sites. To ease this process, make sure to keep all documentation received with components.

◆ To research the latest drivers for Compaq systems and hardware: *http://www.compaq.com/support/index.shtml.*

◆ To research the latest drivers for Dell systems and hardware: *http://support.dell.com/us/en/home.asp.*

◆ To research the latest drivers for Sun systems and hardware: *http://www.sun.com/service/index.html;$sessionid$OSFIGTIAAB1M1AMTA1LU3NQ.*

◆ To research the latest drivers for HP systems and hardware: *http://welcome.hp.com/country/us/eng/software_drivers.htm.*

◆ When downloading drivers, it is important to note that some of these files are large. The technician should be prepared to either download to a hard drive and run a disk creation utility or to download to a floppy if the file is small enough.

◆ Remember, when a driver is updated on a system, often the service pack needs to be reapplied. This also applies when a new device driver is added to an up-and-running server system.

◆ Driver updates should be performed when the server can be rebooted without affecting the network and users. Not all driver updates require a reboot; however, it is common practice to allow ample time for unexpected problems to arise.

◆ Make sure to have a current backup, boot disks, ERDs, and the original OS disks on hand in the event these items become necessary.

OBJECTIVES ON THE JOB

As with updating anything on the server, it is important to note that although the OS of choice is extremely individualized, maintaining current device drivers, updates, patches, supplements, and service packs is roughly the same from OS to OS. Incorrect updates and changes of this nature can result in damage to current settings and specifications. A server technician should employ every precaution to prevent corruption of the OS and loss of data.

PRACTICE TEST QUESTIONS

1. **John is installing a new 3Com network card in a Compaq server with Novell NetWare 5.1 installed. The server was purchased without the NIC. Where is the first place John should look for the latest drivers for the NIC?**
   a. Novell's support site
   b. Compaq's support site
   c. 3Com's site
   d. on the installation disks provided with the original server purchase

2. **After performing an update of a driver for an embedded NIC, Stacey noted that other system devices were not loading on POST. What should Stacey do to find the problem?**
   a. Uninstall the driver and see if the problem goes away.
   b. Update the BIOS.
   c. Reboot the system into the OS.
   d. Update all the other device drivers one at a time to see if the problem goes away.

3. **When updating a driver or application within an NT environment, which of the following should a server technician have prepared in advance?**
   a. latest BIOS update disk
   b. ERD
   c. extra floppies
   d. the latest firmware updates on a floppy

4. **A new external tape device was purchased for a Dell server, which was purchased last year. Richard received a driver with the tape drive. Which of the following statements is true?**
   a. Richard needs to obtain the latest drivers for all other devices on the system in order for the new driver to load properly.
   b. The driver received with the tape drive should be the most up to date and should work fine.
   c. Richard needs to go to the OS software vendor's Web site and download a driver.
   d. Richard should contact Dell technical support and find out if the driver will work.

5. **Which of the following should be performed when planning to update device drivers on a server?**
   a. Schedule server downtime and reboot.
   b. Perform a full system backup.
   c. Have ERDs and original OS disks available.
   d. all of the above

6. **After Susan updated the NIC driver for her Dell system with NT, she noticed that other devices were not recognized on POST. What is the easiest way to fix this problem?**
   a. Reapply the current service pack.
   b. Schedule a hard drive replacement.
   c. Reinstall the operating system.
   d. Purchase a new NIC and load a different driver.

2.7   Install service tools

INSTALL SERVICE TOOLS

UNDERSTANDING THE OBJECTIVE

After the server is physically set up, configured, and then integrated into a client/server network, the next major task a server technician should address is the installation of a method for monitoring and managing the devices on the network from the server. One such method is to install and configure **Simple Network Management Protocol (SNMP)**. This section reviews the highlights of installing this protocol.

Another important task the server technician will complete is the installation of tape backup software. This is crucial to the functionality of the server. Part of the daily routine in a busy server environment is performing backups. This section highlights the major points of the installation.

WHAT YOU REALLY NEED TO KNOW

◆ *SNMP*
Virtually all network routers, hubs, and switches have embedded SNMP capability. SNMP agents are supplied with many OSs, including Windows NT, Sun, HP, DEC, Linux, and many other platforms.
To configure SNMP on a server, administrators must know the "read community" values of SNMP agents on the network. The "read community" is a text string that serves as a password to an SNMP device. The default SNMP read community for many SNMP agents is "public."
After the SNMP is installed and the administrator logs on, the next step is the setup of the socket identification by which the information is discovered. Get requests, get next requests, set requests, and traps are configured here.

◆ *Tape Backup Software*
The primary purpose of using tape backup software is data protection. Although most server OSs employ some type of native backup solution, it is common practice for a server technician to perform the installation of additional, third-party backup software. Depending on the server's OS, the installation should be conducted according to the software vendor's specifications. Make sure your server configuration and hardware specifications meet the requirements outlined by the backup software manufacturers. Veritas is one vendor that provides many versions of Backup Exec to suit the needs of businesses utilizing this type of tape backup software. Often the software installed by server administrators is a standard single-server edition. Agent accelerators are added for remote server backup functionality.

OBJECTIVES ON THE JOB

A fully functional server requires the tools to manage all devices on the network with alerts and monitoring capabilities.

PRACTICE TEST QUESTIONS

1. Which of the following is a protocol/agent that is installed and configured to monitor and manage devices on the same network?
    a. DHCP
    b. SNMP
    c. SMTP
    d. POP3

2. Which of the following is a common read community name for SNMP agents?
    a. root
    b. IP address of the server
    c. calvin
    d. public

3. Becky was configuring SNMP for her NT server. Which of the following can be configured?
    a. get requests
    b. traps
    c. set requests
    d. all of the above

4. SNMP stands for:
    a. Silent Network Management Program
    b. Simple Network Management Protocol
    c. Simple Network Multitasking Program
    d. Silent Node Management Protocol

5. Susan was scheduling the tape backups for the network and realized the native OS's backup software was not keeping accurate schedules of backups. What should she do?
    a. Reinstall the OS and try the backups again.
    b. Apply a patch for the OS and see if that helps the backups.
    c. Update the firmware on the tape drive.
    d. Install a third-party backup software with more advanced capabilities.

6. Which of the following is a vendor of tape backup software?
    a. Symantec
    b. AMD
    c. Veritas
    d. AT&T

7. Jim wanted to install a tape backup software program. Where should he get information on the best way to do this?
    a. backup software vendor's site
    b. OS vendor's site
    c. server manufacturer's site
    d. tape drive manufacturer's site

2.7 Install service tools (continued)

INSTALL SERVICE TOOLS

UNDERSTANDING THE OBJECTIVE

Monitoring the network and the devices attached to the network is crucial to proper server management. Many tools for this are inherent to the OSs used today in server environments. This section highlights configuring system monitoring agents, services, and event logs.

WHAT YOU REALLY NEED TO KNOW

◆ Event logging is used by computer systems to record the occurrence of significant events. An "event" is any change that occurs in a system—for example, a user logon, an addition to a file, or a change to a user's privileges. Because a computer system may experience hundreds or thousands of events each second, it is important to distinguish which events require the immediate attention of a system administrator, which should be recorded as entries in the system's event log for later analysis, and which can be safely ignored.

◆ Error reports, system alerts, diagnostic messages, and status messages generated by a system are part of the following types of NT event logs:

- *Security log*—Stores reports of security-related events; for example, a user has written to a file or a change in a user's privileges.

- *System log*—Stores reports generated by system components, including drivers and services; for example, a device failed, a driver failed to load, or a memory allocation or I/O error occurred.

- *Application log*—Stores reports on all other events; for example, an internal application error (such as a failure to allocate memory) occurred or a file download aborted.

◆ Event logging software is inherent in server OSs and also is available from third-party vendors. Third-party software designed for this should be installed in accordance with the vendor's specifications. It is a good idea to check with the OS vendor and hardware manufacturer for known problematic issues in advance.

◆ System monitoring agents are also available as part of the server OS or as third-party software. HP Openview is one example of a popular third-party software program specifically designed for optimizing server management and both local and remote monitoring. The best method for installing the third-party software is to follow the vendor's recommended installation procedures.

OBJECTIVES ON THE JOB

Server management requires that devices on the network and events occurring on the network be monitored. This ensures that the network and all devices are functioning at optimum levels.

PRACTICE TEST QUESTIONS

1. Daniel was contacted by a user on his network who told him that she could not access files on one of the network file servers. Which of the following should Daniel check for changes in user permissions?
   a. Application log
   b. History log
   c. Event log
   d. Security log

2. To which OS are the System, Application, and Security logs inherent?
   a. NetWare
   b. UNIX
   c. OS/2
   d. Windows NT

3. Bob wanted to know how many times a user had attempted to log on to the server before she was locked out of the network. Which of the following logs should Bob check first?
   a. Application log
   b. History log
   c. Event log
   d. Security log

4. Which tools can a server administrator employ to monitor and manage a network more efficiently?
   a. Application log and SMTP
   b. event logging software and SNMP
   c. event logging software and SMTP
   d. antivirus software and SNMP

5. HP Openview is used for which of the following?
   a. local and remote server management
   b. remote server management only
   c. performing remote backups only
   d. creating an event log only

6. What type of software or service does Bill need to install or configure to receive hardware failure alerts on a server in New York when he is in Austin, Texas?
   a. SNMP
   b. SMTP
   c. POP3
   d. security logging services

OBJECTIVES

2.8 Perform Server baseline

PERFORM SERVER BASELINE

UNDERSTANDING THE OBJECTIVE

A server technician should gather server baseline information on a regular basis. This information is used to analyze system performance. Baseline evaluations should be performed to determine performance on everything from server hardware to network activity. Baselines are very useful tools for troubleshooting. This section highlights the main points of performing a server baseline.

WHAT YOU REALLY NEED TO KNOW

- There are third-party software utilities available for creating server baselines, but most OSs have native utilities for creating server baselines. Generally, a server baseline should be created over three or four days at varying intervals to determine the baseline function of the server throughout varying degrees of system loads.
- When establishing a server baseline, first determine what activities should be measured. Activities to consider measuring include the following:
  - Server utilization
  - Memory usage
  - Disk utilization
  - Processor utilization
- You should also obtain a baseline during peak operations. This baseline identifies bottlenecks and provides you with the necessary information to determine which server components should be upgraded.
- View the information from your baseline thoroughly. High percentages of utilization can identify hardware problems and software configuration issues.
- Before attempting to upgrade server hardware, you should check to see if your OS is configured correctly. Many bottlenecks can be resolved by optimizing settings in your OS. For example, creating a larger paging file or moving the paging file across multiple drives may resolve problems with memory. Your software vendor has additional information to assist you with optimization.
- If a hardware upgrade is required, a baseline should be performed after the upgrade to ensure that desired results were obtained.

OBJECTIVES ON THE JOB

Server reliability is the main goal of the server administrator. By utilizing the tools that are native to the server OS as well as third-party monitoring software, problems and issues can be resolved. Remember that the baseline state for the server helps you determine whether there is a problem in the first place. This is why you create the server baseline.

PRACTICE TEST QUESTIONS

1. **Of the following, which is the best time to perform a server baseline?**
    a. on the weekends, when no users are logged on to the network
    b. only during the busiest times of the network
    c. anytime, as long as there is a baseline
    d. varying times over an extended period of time (three or four days)

2. **What is the purpose of performing a server baseline?**
    a. to provide the administrator with a benchmark to evaluate system performance and determine problem areas
    b. to gather information on system devices
    c. to monitor the users' activities on the network
    d. to evaluate software updates

3. **Ed was scheduled to perform an upgrade to the processor on one of the main servers on the network. He is not sure whether he needs to perform another server baseline because he just performed one two weeks ago. What should Ed do?**
    a. He does not need to perform another baseline; the one from two weeks ago should provide any data he needs to determine bottleneck activity.
    b. As long as he documents the upgrade, he only needs to perform a one-day server baseline.
    c. He should perform a regular, full server baseline anytime a change is made to the server, especially a processor upgrade.
    d. He should wait to install the new processor until the server needs another one.

4. **A _____ is used to describe a delay in transmission of data through a system's processor or network.**
    a. utilization error
    b. SNMP alert
    c. RAM overload error
    d. bottleneck

5. **Robin wanted to determine if the server she was managing was properly handling logging requests of users. Which log should she review?**
    a. Application
    b. History
    c. Error
    d. Security

6. **What is one method, using setting optimization, to address problems with memory?**
    a. Create a larger paging file.
    b. Add an additional hard drive.
    c. Create another partition and mark it as active.
    d. Clear the cache on the motherboard.

2.9   Document the configuration

DOCUMENT THE CONFIGURATION

UNDERSTANDING THE OBJECTIVE

The purpose of documenting the configuration of the server and its peripherals is to minimize the time required for troubleshooting and gathering information in the future. It is very important to document everything possible about the server configuration. This section emphasizes the major areas to be considered.

WHAT YOU REALLY NEED TO KNOW

- ◆ Everything about the installation should be documented. Detailed information about what was actually done to the server to prepare it for installation and information about the environment are especially helpful. For example, if special wiring was needed to install the server in a particular area, that information may be crucial in the future.

- ◆ Any calls made for support during the installation should also be documented. For example, noting where a driver or patch was received may help to determine a conflict source in the future.

- ◆ It is also a good idea to document where equipment, such as cabling, was obtained. This may prevent repetitive issues regarding faulty equipment.

- ◆ Be sure to document the location of all sources of all equipment. Equipment manufacturers may be difficult to locate in the future; if the equipment is specialized, it is even more crucial to document this information.

- ◆ Try to log all problematic issues (for example, a temperature issue in the room or fluctuations in power without surge protection/line conditioning).

- ◆ It is important to always document the source for any patches, updates, fixes, drivers, and so on.

- ◆ You should keep all certificate and license information in a secure location with appropriate access for those who may need to utilize that information. A special file should be created for this type of documentation; furthermore, a duplicate of this file should be kept in an offsite storage location in the event damage occurs to the original configuration and a recreation becomes necessary.

- ◆ Document who has access to the server for security purposes and make sure the appropriate people have access to that information.

- ◆ You should keep documentation of any problematic issues that have come up since the beginning of the server setup process.

OBJECTIVES ON THE JOB

Documenting the processes and issues incurred during the server setup and management phase is an ongoing task. This lessens the time required to gather information on how problematic issues should be handled.

PRACTICE TEST QUESTIONS

1. **Thomas reviewed the material about the server he manages and discovered that initially, the server was configured with a legacy NIC, which required a specific IRQ configuration. Which of the following statements is the most accurate regarding the original server setup documentation?**
   a. If the system BIOS and IRQ configuration has not changed and the legacy NIC is not in use, additional resources may be available.
   b. The legacy NIC configuration has no effect on the current configuration.
   c. The previous configuration affects Thomas only if he tries to install another NIC.
   d. The previous setup affects Thomas only if he tries to reinstall the OS.

2. **Jim has been receiving some strange errors regarding a Novell file that is needed when trying to update his NT server. Where can Jim go to find out what the problem might be?**
   a. Novell's Web site
   b. the Security log on the NT server
   c. the initial server installation documentation, where he will find out that the server was initially installed as a Novell server but that the hard drive was not formatted before the NT installation
   d. OS CD help files

3. **Which of the following should Chris document for future reference on the server he is managing?**
   a. updates to the server
   b. BIOS/firmware flashes
   c. driver updates to the RAID controller
   d. all of the above

4. **Susan is going to add a new RAID controller and three new hard drives to the server she manages. Which of the following statements is true?**
   a. Susan should log only the information about the RAID controller.
   b. Susan should log all information about adding a new RAID controller and all information about the three new hard drives.
   c. As long as Susan allows the system to recognize the RAID controller on POST, she does not need to document the steps she has taken to load it.
   d. Susan should log only the information about the hard drives.

5. **While Sam and Dave were installing OSs on multiple servers, they noticed that some of the OS software had not been installed on the servers. What may help determine who had access to the area the week they were working on this project?**
   a. documentation regarding access to servers and equipment
   b. video surveillance of the server area at night
   c. checking with security about access to the server room when they were not on site
   d. none of the above

3.1   Perform full backup

VERIFY BACKUP

UNDERSTANDING THE OBJECTIVE

Running a full backup is one of the most important tasks you can perform to ensure data recovery when a disaster occurs. You must understand the procedures involved in performing a full backup and verification.

WHAT YOU REALLY NEED TO KNOW

◆ A **full backup** should be performed before attempting to upgrade or make any other changes to a server.

◆ Full backups are normally implemented with other backup strategies, such as **differential backups**, which back up all data since the last full backup, or **incremental backups**, which back up all data that has changed since the last full backup. Most organizations implement either an incremental or differential backup strategy to ensure maximum recovery in the event of data loss.

◆ A full backup should be scheduled to run at a time when all users are logged off the server. This ensures that important files are closed and completely backed up.

◆ Some backup software packages have scheduling utilities that enable you to perform backups at a specific time. By using the scheduling utility, you can schedule the time and type of backup to be performed. You should take into consideration that a full backup takes quite a bit of time to complete and may require multiple tapes.

◆ The backup process consists of executing the program for your backup software and selecting the available options. You must choose the location of the files to be backed up and the target location of the files, normally your tape backup unit. You may have an option to verify the backup; if so, you should do this after the backup is complete. After the backup process begins, you can see which files are being backed up.

◆ Third-party vendors design backup software that is used by many organizations. You must be familiar with the backup software your organization uses for its backups.

◆ After completing a full backup, you must verify the backup to ensure that it was successful. Verifying a backup involves actually restoring data from the backup media and can identify problems with the tape or problems backing up specific files.

◆ After verifying that the full backup was successful, you should properly label the tapes from the full backup set to ensure that the tapes are not accidentally mixed with a different set of backups.

OBJECTIVES ON THE JOB

Performing a full backup is one of the best defenses you have when the unexpected occurs. By scheduling backups at the appropriate time and developing a backup strategy, you ensure that your organization's data is protected and can be recovered, if necessary. There is a mix of third-party and native backup software on the market. You should consider which features of your backup software could be used to better assist your organization.

PRACTICE TEST QUESTIONS

1. **Charles needs to update a service pack on the server. What should Charles do?**
   a. Upgrade the service pack right away.
   b. Perform an incremental backup.
   c. Perform a full backup.
   d. Shut down the server and upgrade the service pack.

2. **When is the best time to perform a full backup?**
   a. right before users arrive for work
   b. during lunch
   c. one hour after users arrive for work
   d. after users have gone home for the day

3. **John has just completed a full backup of the server. What should he do next?**
   a. Verify the backup.
   b. Rewind the tape.
   c. Set the write-protect tab on the tape.
   d. Change the compression on the tape backup unit.

4. **John is having problems verifying a tape backup. After trying to verify the tape several times, John notices that the tape is failing in the same location. What is most likely causing the problem?**
   a. The tape backup unit needs to be cleaned.
   b. The tape backup unit driver is bad.
   c. There is a problem with the SCSI cable.
   d. The backup tape is bad.

5. **Which of the following can be implemented with full backups to ensure data recovery? (Choose all that apply.)**
   a. incremental backups
   b. half-duplex backups
   c. differential backups
   d. partial backups

6. **A full backup _____ (Choose all that apply.)**
   a. takes more time to complete than other backups
   b. takes less time to complete than other backups
   c. should be verified after completion
   d. never needs more than one tape to complete

7. **Barbara performed a full backup of the server on Sunday and incremental backups for the rest of the week. The server failed on Thursday and must be restored from tape. How many backup sets does Barbara need to restore the server?**
   a. 3
   b. 4
   c. 2
   d. 5

3.2 Add processors

**ON SINGLE PROCESSOR UPGRADE, VERIFY COMPATIBILITY • VERIFY N 1
STEPPING • VERIFY SPEED AND CACHE MATCHING**

UNDERSTANDING THE OBJECTIVE

To upgrade a single CPU or processor successfully, you should verify the compatibility of the motherboard and the processor. It is highly recommended that you research information about the processor and motherboard via the hardware manufacturer, the Web, manuals, and CDs. If you fail to perform this crucial step, the damage to the CPU and motherboard can be costly. You should always back up data before upgrading.

WHAT YOU REALLY NEED TO KNOW

◆ You should verify compatibility for the type of motherboard and new processor, keeping in mind the following possible differences:
  - Number of pins/type of socket—Research the type of socket you have to ensure that the processor is compatible with the motherboard.
  - Pinouts—The actual function of each pin. For example, the DX and SX processors both have 168 pins, but they have different pinouts. This means that different pins carry different signals to the processor.
  - Voltage—Proper voltage must be supplied for reliable operation. Voltage regulators are helpful in certain instances. For example, the operating voltage of Intel Celeron processors may be changed as the processor goes through stepping changes (such as with BIOS upgrades), thereby causing a fluctuation in the voltage requirements. Also, improper voltage management can lead to the processor overheating and potential damage to your equipment.
  - Speed—Proper matching of processor speed for the motherboard is imperative. Check with the motherboard's manufacturer regarding the optimal solution.
  - Stepping—(also called S-spec) Processors have a module number and a major and minor stepping version. For example, an Intel Pentium II Xeon with 32 K cache has a major stepping version of 73726 and a minor stepping version of (5). For processors to be compatible, the major stepping version must be the same and the minor stepping version must be within one version (that is, if the minor stepping version is 5, then a processor with a minor stepping version of 4 or 6 is acceptable). This is known as N (+/-) 1 stepping.
  - Primary or L1 cache—Usually built into the architecture of microprocessors and typically 16 K. The Intel 80486 microprocessor, for example, contains an 8 K memory cache, and the Pentium has a 16 K cache. Memory caching is effective because most programs access the same data or instructions over and over.

OBJECTIVES ON THE JOB

Processor upgrades are a common procedure for a server technician; you should be familiar with the current terminology and technology available for processors and motherboards to ensure a comprehensive understanding of the upgrade options available for your business.

PRACTICE TEST QUESTIONS

1. **What does the term "L1 cache" refer to?**
   a. additional memory on the motherboard
   b. additional disk space on the hard drive
   c. integrated memory on the CPU
   d. level one disk arrays

2. **While Robert was planning the upgrade of the server's processor, he noted that the documentation from the initial installation does not include any of the specifications about the processor. Which of the following will *not* provide Robert with information about the processor's specifications?**
   a. the system BIOS
   b. the RAID controller's BIOS
   c. CDs/manuals that may have been shipped with the original parts
   d. the Web

3. **What is the physical difference between the SX and DX processor?**
   a. different number of pins
   b. different L1 cache
   c. The number of pins is the same; the signals carried by the pins are different.
   d. Different sockets are required.

4. **Debbie was about to perform a processor upgrade on the server. Which of the following should she verify for compatibility? (Choose all that apply.)**
   a. drivers
   b. stepping
   c. speed
   d. manufacturer

5. **When installing multiple processors, the processors must have the same _____. (Choose all that apply.)**
   a. stepping
   b. cache
   c. RAID
   d. all of the above

6. **What must every technician do before performing any upgrade procedure?**
   a. Check power supplies.
   b. Verify speed, cache, and stepping.
   c. Schedule downtime and notify users.
   d. Back up all data.

3.2 Add processors (continued)

PERFORM BIOS UPGRADE

UNDERSTANDING THE OBJECTIVE

It often becomes necessary to upgrade your system's BIOS. The term "BIOS" refers to the system's internal set of instructions within the CMOS on how to communicate with, test, and load the devices attached to it. Driver updates and hardware upgrades often create a need to perform a BIOS flash. The term "flash" is used for actually transferring the new set of instructions to your system. When upgrading your system's processor and/or motherboard, it is common to flash the BIOS with the most current BIOS available from the motherboard manufacturer. Failing to perform the upgrade can result in system inoperability, loss of certain functions the processor may have been enhanced to perform (such as advanced mathematical calculations), and other errors.

WHAT YOU REALLY NEED TO KNOW

- ◆ Step 1: Identify the BIOS type—Determine the make of your BIOS/motherboard. Some BIOS versions include the version date in the identifier string on your boot screen.
- ◆ Step 2: Contact the manufacturer—Using the results from Step 1, contact your BIOS (or motherboard) manufacturer to see if an update is available for your motherboard/BIOS. Obtain a copy of it, if one is available.
- ◆ Step 3: Prepare the system and network—Write down all current CMOS settings and specifications. Make sure that you back up all data and that the recovery plan is in place. Schedule to perform the upgrade at a time that will not impact users. Also note that components with their own BIOS may require an update if you flash the system's BIOS. Check the documentation available on specific devices/controllers to find out how to perform this step. OS service packs may also require reapplication after these updates are performed. Check with the software vendors to find out if this is the case.
- ◆ Step 4: Apply the upgrade (flash)—Perform this step only when your power source is stable, not during electrical storms. Use the instructions provided by the manufacturer, and follow the steps required to run the BIOS update.
- ◆ Step 5: Check the system after the BIOS update is completed—Go into CMOS Setup (indicated from your boot screen) to ensure that all information is correct and that the version has updated. Use your system to make sure there are no upgrade-related problems.

OBJECTIVES ON THE JOB

When it becomes necessary to flash your system's BIOS, many resources are available to assist you via the Web. Motherboard and processor manufacturers regularly post updates and revision information for their products, as well as helpful instructions for performing these upgrades.

PRACTICE TEST QUESTIONS

1. John installed a new processor on the motherboard from the previous server. He verified the compatibility of the sockets as well as the speed, cache, and stepping. To ensure complete functionality of the new processor on the "old" motherboard, what should he do next?

    a. Flash the BIOS of the motherboard.
    b. Flash the BIOS of the RAID controller.
    c. Perform a backup of all data.
    d. Upgrade the cache on the motherboard.

2. After installing a processor on a previously used motherboard, Jean noticed errors with certain mathematical applications. What should Jean do first to try to eliminate the errors?

    a. Upgrade all drivers.
    b. Flash the BIOS of the RAID controller.
    d. Reinstall the operating system.
    d. Flash the BIOS of the motherboard.

3. Another technician has installed a new processor, and Stephen has been instructed to flash the BIOS. He has not done this before and does not have a walk-through guide on how to do this. What resources does Stephen have available to find this information? (Choose all that apply.)

    a. the Web
    b. hard drive manufacturer's technical support
    c. motherboard manufacturer's technical support
    d. hardware specification manuals

4. The system's BIOS is directly related to the _____

    a. RAID BIOS
    b. CMOS
    c. RAID controller
    d. network infrastructure

5. Which of the following tasks is *not* required prior to performing a BIOS upgrade?

    a. Write down all current CMOS settings and specifications. Make sure that you back up all data and that the recovery plan is in place. Schedule to perform the upgrade at a time that will not impact users.
    b. Update all system drivers.
    c. Determine the manufacturer of your BIOS/motherboard.
    d. Go into CMOS Setup (indicated from your boot screen) to make certain all information is correct and that the version has updated. Use your system to make sure there are no upgrade-related problems.

3.2   Add processors (continued)

PERFORM OS UPGRADE TO SUPPORT MULTIPROCESSORS • PERFORM UPGRADE CHECKLIST

UNDERSTANDING THE OBJECTIVE

Prior to installing a second processor into a single-processor system, it is important to find out if the version of the operating system and the settings within it support a multiple-processor environment. There are various techniques for performing this procedure. Once the second processor is recognized by the system, you should perform a baseline to ensure functionality of the system's devices and enhancements. Creating an upgrade checklist should be a part of every technician's role when upgrading any device. In this section, we highlight specific areas to check when performing a processor upgrade.

WHAT YOU REALLY NEED TO KNOW

◆ Before performing a processor upgrade on any system, you should review both hardware and software specifications as outlined by each manufacturer.

◆ You should check with your software vendor for instructions and specifications regarding multiple-processor usage with your specific operating system. Not all operating systems support a multiple processor environment.

◆ To upgrade a single-processor Windows NT system to a multiprocessor system, use Uptomp.exe. Uptomp.exe is included in the resource kit for Windows NT version 3.5.

◆ An upgrade checklist helps you verify that all stages of the upgrade have been completed. It also provides an outline to document the specific outcome of the various changes performed on the system. This is especially helpful if future troubleshooting is required.

◆ An upgrade checklist should include the following tasks:

1. Gather needed information, including BIOS versions, manufacturer information, and hardware specifications.

2. Obtain the BIOS flash and system/OS updates necessary, along with instructions/suggestions on how to install them.

3. Prepare the system and network by scheduling downtime, detaching external peripherals, notifying users, and so on.

4. Check the system after the BIOS update is complete. Enter the CMOS Setup (indicated from your boot screen) to make certain that all information is correct and that the version has updated. Use your system to make sure that there are no upgrade-related problems.

5. Document all events and issues that came up during the process.

OBJECTIVES ON THE JOB

By following the steps outlined in this section, you should be able to perform processor upgrades, update the OS to recognize a second processor, and create an upgrade checklist.

PRACTICE TEST QUESTIONS

1. **Gene installed a second processor in his system. Upon completing his upgrade checklist, he realizes he needs to upgrade his operating system to recognize the new processor. Where should he get the instructions on how to *best* complete this task?**
   a. server manufacturer's Web site
   b. upgrade checklist/documentation
   c. software vendor
   d. BIOS help files

2. **What are some reasons for performing an upgrade checklist? (Choose all that apply.)**
   a. to support a multiprocessor configuration
   b. to verify that all steps have been completed successfully for the upgrade
   c. to minimize future troubleshooting
   d. to update all system drivers

3. **Installing multiple processors may require updating the server's _____.**
   a. RAID controller
   b. network adapter
   c. operating system
   d. none of the above

4. **James is gathering the information needed to perform a processor upgrade on a server with an older motherboard. What information is *not* needed in this phase?**
   a. updated drivers
   b. current BIOS version
   c. BIOS flash data from the manufacturer
   d. current CMOS settings

5. **What is *one* reason you should verify that the operating system you are working with has been configured to work in a multiple-processor environment?**
   a. to avoid a reinstallation of the operating system's service pack
   b. to ensure that the RAID controller can accept the increased demand
   c. to avoid having to update all system drivers
   d. The system may not utilize the processor, thereby decreasing the effectiveness of your investment and the overall processing power of the system itself.

6. **Which of the following is an example of a utility designed to upgrade a Windows operating system from single-processor to multiprocessor capabilities?**
   a. Uptome.exe
   b. Uptomp.exe
   c. Msupgrade.exe
   d. Upgrade.exe

3.3 Add hard drives

VERIFY THAT DRIVES ARE THE APPROPRIATE TYPE • CONFIRM TERMINATION AND CABLING

UNDERSTANDING THE OBJECTIVE

The main purpose for installing new hard drives is to increase storage capacity. There are many other areas to consider when choosing the appropriate type of hard drive based on the current server hardware configuration and your company's needs.

WHAT YOU REALLY NEED TO KNOW

- ◆ No other hardware failure can lead to disaster more readily than a hard drive failure. Because of this, hard drive quality and reliability are the two main features you should consider when choosing a hard drive.

- ◆ **Mean time between failures (MTBF)** is a common term used when discussing the quality and reliability of hard drive performance. It is a value, usually measured in hours, that represents the average amount of time that will pass between random failures on a drive of a given type. It is usually in the range of 300,000 to 1.2 million hours for modern drives (with the range increasing every few years) and is specified for almost every drive.

- ◆ The following is a list of hard drive features and specifications:

  - Size—Hard drives usually come in 3 1/2-inch and 5 1/4-inch sizes. Verify what size hard drive bay and hard drive enclosure you need to choose the correct size.

  - Interface—Hard drives are IDE/ATA, SCSI, or FC. Choose the interface type that matches the interface and controller you have available on your system. If installing a SCSI hard drive, note that termination of the device is necessary to prevent signal bounce on the SCSI bus. This can be set manually using jumpers on the hard drive itself or may be set automatically via the SCSI controller. Termination also can be completed by using a terminator on the cable. Also, the interface and controller determine what type of cabling is necessary to install your hard drive(s). Make sure to use the appropriate cabling to avoid damage to the drive and the controller.

  - Speed—Usually specified in revolutions per minute (RPMs).

  - Storage capacity—Specified in megabytes (MB) and gigabytes (GB).

  - Special features—Major hard drive manufacturers offer special features, such as failure prediction technology, special noise reduction, and temperature control.

OBJECTIVES ON THE JOB

One of the most common tasks of a server technician involves hard drive technology. You should be familiar with the hard drive specifications and optimal product performance standards to ensure that your system is performing as it should.

PRACTICE TEST QUESTIONS

1. **Robert is planning an upgrade for the server's IDE hard drives. He is considering purchasing four SCSI drives because the warranty offered with them is outstanding. What else should Robert consider when planning this upgrade? (Choose all that apply.)**
   a. the increased network load on the system
   b. the size of the drives
   c. the termination of the drives
   d. controller/cabling because he's changing from IDE to SCSI drives

2. **What is the term used to define the quality and reliability of a hard disk drive in regard to performance?**
   a. RAID
   b. MTBF
   c. RPMs
   d. IDE/ATA

3. **Which of the following are hard drive features and/or specifications? (Choose all that apply.)**
   a. failure prediction technology
   b. RPMs
   c. storage capacity
   d. stepping

4. **Debbie is about to perform a hard drive upgrade on the server. Which of the following should she verify for compatibility? (Choose all that apply.)**
   a. drivers
   b. interface/cabling
   c. size
   d. manufacturer

5. **The main purpose for installing new hard drives is to increase _____.**
   a. storage capacity
   b. cache memory
   c. failure prediction
   d. data access

6. **What is the most important thing a server technician should do to prevent loss of data?**
   a. Purchase drives capable of failure prediction.
   b. Verify speed, size, and cabling of drives.
   c. Increase storage capacity of drives.
   d. Back up all data.

3.3 Add hard drives (continued)

FOR ATA/IDE DRIVES, CONFIRM CABLING, MASTER/SLAVE AND POTENTIAL CROSS-BRAND COMPATIBILITY

UNDERSTANDING THE OBJECTIVE

AT Attachment/Integrated Drive Electronics (ATA/IDE) is the most popular hard drive interface in the PC world. It is also very common in the server environment, especially because many new Internet appliances are being scaled down in size as well as cost.

WHAT YOU REALLY NEED TO KNOW

- The master/slave setting allows you to have two drives attached to the same controller. The first drive attached to the data cable is usually the master, and the second drive attached to that cable is the slave. Most new drives come set to be the master by default. If you are replacing a single existing drive, or if you are connecting the new drive to a second controller, you usually don't need to make any changes.

- If you are adding the drive to a controller to which you have already attached the existing drive, you will want to set your new drive as the slave. Usually, this involves changing a jumper. Jumper pins are located on the hard drive itself. To change the jumper position from master to slave, remove it from the master position pins and place it over the slave position pins. Refer to the manufacturer's documentation for the specific details for the drive you have purchased.

- Incorrectly changing a jumper for the drives can cause the server not to boot or to display a message indicating that no operating system is available, even though the previous hard drive (with an OS on it) is still intact.

- When upgrading ATA/IDE drives, ensure that the drives are compatible with the drives already installed. Check with the hardware vendors for compatibility issues.

- Connect the cable so that the colored stripe matches up with the 0/1 pins on the motherboard. Your motherboard should be imprinted with the 0/1 designation so that it is easy to see where the striped side of the cable should connect.

- Connect the other end of the data cable to the back of the hard drive, again matching the striped side of the cable with the 0/1 pin position on the drive itself. Be sure to check the hard drive you purchased to see which direction the red stripe should go. IDE drives do not require termination; SCSI drives do.

OBJECTIVES ON THE JOB

ATA/IDE drive replacement is a job skill with which server technicians should be familiar. Individual drive jumpers are specific to the manufacturer of that drive and should be researched before attempting to change a jumper. Compatibility issues are also a concern when upgrading to newer drives, so this also should be researched prior to installing the new hard drives. As a field technician, you can perform this task with fewer complications by following the suggestions above.

PRACTICE TEST QUESTIONS

1. **John is going to install a new IDE hard drive on the server. He notes that the new hard drive is larger than the previous one and decides that it is better used as a master. What must John do to the *new* drive to ensure that it will serve as the master drive?**
   a. No action is required other than verification, because most drives are set to serve as the master by default.
   b. He needs to manually change the jumper settings on the old drive to ensure that it is set as the master.
   c. He needs to manually change the jumper settings on the new drive to ensure that it is set as the slave.
   d. He needs to change the settings from slave to master in the CMOS for the new drive.

2. **What must John do to the cable to ensure that the new drive is recognized as the master drive?**
   a. Place the old drive on the first position on the cable.
   b. Set termination on the drive after the first position.
   c. Place the new drive on the first position on the cable.
   d. Place the new drive on the second position on the cable with termination.

3. **Using the scenario in Question 1, choose the correct answer regarding terminating the new IDE drive:**
   a. John should place the new drive on the second position on the cable with termination.
   b. Termination is not applicable since it is an IDE controller/drive.
   c. The jumpers need to be set on the drive to terminate the drive.
   d. John should place a terminator on the end of the cable to terminate the chain.

4. **On an ATA/IDE hard drive, the jumpers are located _____.**
   a. in the CMOS
   b. on the motherboard
   c. on the RAID controller
   d. on the hard drive

5. **Bill installed a new IDE hard drive on the server. The previous hard drive contained data and an OS that he recently backed up. Upon reboot, he receives an error message that no operating system is available. What should he check *first* to resolve this issue?**
   a. motherboard jumpers
   b. BIOS version
   c. master/slave configuration
   d. termination

3.3 Add hard drives (continued)

UPGRADE MASS STORAGE • ADD DRIVES TO ARRAY • REPLACE EXISTING DRIVES • INTEGRATE INTO STORAGE SOLUTION AND MAKE IT AVAILABLE TO THE OPERATING SYSTEM • PERFORM UPGRADE CHECKLIST

UNDERSTANDING THE OBJECTIVE

Upgrading mass storage can encompass many areas. Because mass storage indicates the use of multiple drives, a SCSI controller or RAID controller is necessary. This, in turn, indicates a hardware or software RAID array. When the physical upgrade is complete, changes must be made to utilize the additional data storage space. You should always review your upgrade checklist to ensure that no steps have been missed.

WHAT YOU REALLY NEED TO KNOW

◆ Before making any changes or additions (such as adding new drives), always perform a full system backup and verify the backup.

◆ Mass storage devices contain multiple hard drives. These hard drives are normally configured as part of a RAID array.

◆ When adding hard drives to an array, all drives in the array should be identical to avoid adverse effects on the array, such as a loss of all the data on the drives. Labeling the drives as you remove them (if you remove them) is extremely important.

◆ RAID controllers have their own BIOS, which is accessible during the boot process. By entering the BIOS and making drive changes, you can add the new drives into existing arrays and reconfigure the arrays.

◆ SCSI controllers also have their own BIOS. Access the drives to assign/view SCSI ID information as well as perform functions such as formatting.

◆ Refer to your RAID controller documentation on how to access the drive configuration menus. Make sure that you understand how to work with a RAID array before making any changes to prevent loss of data.

◆ Note that after you have added hard drives and created a new array, you must partition and format the drive space to make it available to your operating system. This can be performed from within the RAID controller's BIOS or from within the OS (NT- Disk Administrator).

◆ An upgrade checklist helps you to verify that all stages of an upgrade have been performed and that the system functions as expected afterward. The checklist should include installation of current drivers, OS updates, scheduled downtime, and baseline review.

OBJECTIVES ON THE JOB

As a server technician, it is imperative that you become familiar with storage management. When an upgrade is performed, you will be required to understand how to effectively assign and use the drive space you are adding.

PRACTICE TEST QUESTIONS

1. **Chris installed five 9 GB drives and created a RAID 5 array. After installing NT 4.0, Chris only sees a 4 GB partition and 32 GB of disk space in Disk Administrator. What should Chris do to access the rest of his disk space?**
   a. Partition and format the free space in Disk Administrator.
   b. Remove and reconfigure the array.
   c. Boot to a bootable DOS diskette and format the remaining free space.
   d. Flash the BIOS on the RAID controller.

2. **When planning a mass storage upgrade on his RAID 5 array, John planned to perform the following steps: research the drive type, configuration, and installation procedure; install the new drives; and review the upgrade checklist for adding mass storage devices. What very important step is missing?**
   a. obtain the BIOS updates
   b. perform a full system backup/verification of data
   c. contact the manufacturer for drivers
   d. notify users of downtime

3. **RAID and SCSI controllers have their own _____.**
   a. stepping
   b. BIOS
   c. arrays
   d. sockets

4. **Debbie installed new hard drives in the server. She needs to reformat the drives. How can she access the drives if there is no operating system on the server?**
   a. through the CMOS
   b. through Disk Administrator
   c. through the SCSI or RAID controller's BIOS, which is accessible during the boot process
   d. through Disk Manager

5. **After you have added hard drives and created a new array, you must _____ the drive space to make it available to your operating system.**
   a. create and format
   b. install and format
   c. format and confirm
   d. partition and format

3.4 Increase memory

VERIFY HARDWARE AND OS SUPPORT FOR CAPACITY INCREASE • VERIFY MEMORY IS ON HARDWARE/VENDOR COMPATIBILITY LIST • VERIFY MEMORY COMPATIBILITY • PERFORM UPGRADE CHECKLIST • VERIFY THAT SERVER AND OS RECOGNIZE THE ADDED MEMORY • PERFORM SERVER OPTIMIZATION TO MAKE USE OF ADDITIONAL RAM

UNDERSTANDING THE OBJECTIVE

Upgrading memory is one of the easiest ways to increase the overall performance of the system. By understanding this process, you can ensure that your server will take advantage of the extra memory.

WHAT YOU REALLY NEED TO KNOW

◆ Before performing a memory upgrade, determine whether your server has available memory slots. Ensure that the motherboard supports the additional memory. You may be required to flash the BIOS before adding **Random Access Memory (RAM)**.

◆ Most servers only accept a specific type and size of memory. Check with your server vendor to ensure memory compatibility. (You should check the HCL.)

◆ When adding memory, always ensure that the memory is the same type, speed, and brand as the memory currently in use.

◆ When installing memory, ensure that you are properly grounded. ESD can damage memory modules. Also ensure that the memory is properly seated in its slot.

◆ After the memory has been installed, you must verify that the server recognizes the additional memory. You can see the memory count when the system POSTs.

◆ Memory should also be verified in the server's SSU. Not verifying and saving the change can result in errors at POST.

◆ If your legacy system runs an **Extended Industry Standard Architecture (EISA)** Configuration utility, that utility must be run to update the RAM count.

◆ The OS should recognize the additional memory installed. Some OSs require a patch to recognize large amounts of memory. You should be able to view the necessary information in the System Resource area of your OS.

◆ After you have successfully installed additional memory, document the configuration changes so you'll have the most current information available for future reference.

◆ After the server has been optimized to increase performance, a server baseline should be run and evaluated to ensure that all objectives were accomplished.

◆ An upgrade checklist verifies that all steps have been accomplished, such as BIOS setting, system recognition, OS upgrade, downtime scheduling, and baseline review.

OBJECTIVES ON THE JOB

Adding memory to a server is a common task. You should become familiar with the types of memory and their compatibility across different server platforms and OSs.

PRACTICE TEST QUESTIONS

1. **Which of the following is important when adding memory to a server?**
   a. memory type
   b. speed
   c. OS
   d. all of the above

2. **After memory has been installed, the _____ must be run to update the server's configuration.**
   a. SSU
   b. Disk Administrator
   c. POST Enumerator
   d. EMI utility

3. **Why should you perform a server baseline after installing additional memory?**
   a. to check the parity of the memory slots
   b. to verify that the CMOS settings are correct
   c. to ensure that the upgrade has increased performance of the server
   d. to clear the memory buffer registry

4. **Jim added two 128 MB DIMMs to his server. When he tries to boot the server, the server will not POST. When Jim removes the memory, the server boots with no problems. What could cause this problem?**
   a. The DIMMs are not seated properly.
   b. The DIMM(s) are bad.
   c. The DIMMs are not compatible with the server.
   d. all of the above

5. **Chuck just added 4 GB of RAM to his server. Chuck verified the RAM in the SSU and at POST. When Chuck boots the server, the OS only shows the 1 GB of memory that was previously installed in the system. What is the possible answer to Chuck's problem?**
   a. The memory is not properly seated in the slot.
   b. The system BIOS needs to be flashed.
   c. The OS needs to be patched to update software capabilities.
   d. RAMDRIVE needs to be run on the server.

6. **John has just installed four identical 64 MB DIMMs in a legacy server. After completing the installation, he receives the following message at POST: "F1 to Continue, F2 to run System Setup." John sees the correct amount of memory and saves the settings. At POST, John receives the same message. What is a possible solution to the problem?**
   a. Run the SSU and manually input the memory size.
   b. Do nothing. This is not an error.
   c. Remove and reinstall the CMOS battery.
   d. Run the EISA Configuration utility to update system settings.

OBJECTIVES

3.5 Upgrade BIOS/firmware

PERFORM UPGRADE CHECKLIST

UNDERSTANDING THE OBJECTIVE

Manufacturers are constantly looking for ways to improve the performance of hardware. Those improvements are implemented by updating the BIOS and/or firmware. As a technician, you must know the procedures involved with updating the BIOS and/or firmware.

WHAT YOU REALLY NEED TO KNOW

- ◆ You should always ensure that you have the most current BIOS/firmware specific to your server's configuration. BIOS/firmware revisions are at times solutions to problems you may be experiencing with hardware and software.

- ◆ A BIOS/firmware upgrade should be considered a major operation. Always thoroughly plan a BIOS/firmware upgrade. You should ask yourself the following questions before attempting the upgrade:

  1. Is the server a mission-critical server?

  2. Do I have a full backup of the server in case the upgrade fails or causes problems?

  3. Have I scheduled the appropriate time to perform the upgrade?

  4. Do I have the correct BIOS/firmware revision for my system?

- ◆ Verify that the BIOS/firmware is compatible with your server, installed hardware, and software. Check for known issues and FAQs on the vendor's Web site before attempting the upgrade. Your current BIOS revision can be verified when the server boots or by entering the BIOS during system startup. The firmware revision for a device (tape drive, RAID controller, and so on) is normally displayed under system information for the device.

- ◆ The BIOS or firmware upgrade will be located on the vendor's Web site. The upgrade package gives a description of the BIOS, the version, upgrades or problems the update fixed, and specific instructions for performing the upgrade. The file is normally an executable file that creates diskettes for the actual upgrade.

- ◆ Never power off a server or interrupt the flash process during the upgrade. Doing so could render your system inoperable and result in having to replace the motherboard or hardware.

- ◆ After you have updated the BIOS or firmware, always verify that the revision installed successfully and document the system changes for future reference.

OBJECTIVES ON THE JOB

When given the task of performing a BIOS or firmware upgrade, consider all the factors surrounding the process. Carefully plan the upgrade and ensure that you have all the necessary tools and information to complete the upgrade successfully.

PRACTICE TEST QUESTIONS

1. **Which of the following should be considered before performing a BIOS/firmware upgrade? (Choose all that apply.)**
   a. compatibility
   b. server role
   c. users
   d. network type

2. **Gary is performing an inventory of all servers in a department. As part of the inventory, Gary must record the BIOS revision level on each server. Where can Gary view this information? (Choose all that apply.)**
   a. in the server boot process
   b. in the BIOS
   c. on the back of the server
   d. on the frame inside the server chassis

3. **Kevin has been given the task of upgrading the server BIOS. Where can Kevin find the correct BIOS revision for his system?**
   a. on the OS CDs
   b. on the server vendor's Web site
   c. on the OS vendor's Web site
   d. none of the above

4. **John has to upgrade the tape backup unit's firmware. The upgrade instructions that John downloaded reference files contained on two diskettes. The only file John downloaded was a file named FM18362.exe. What should John do?**
   a. Call the vendor and inform them that their site has a problem.
   b. Search the vendor's Web site for the files that the instructions reference.
   c. Execute the file to create the diskettes referenced in the instructions.
   d. Delete the file and attempt to download it again.

5. **Sharon just upgraded the server BIOS. Which of the following tasks should be performed? (Choose all that apply.)**
   a. Verify that the BIOS updated successfully.
   b. Document the upgrade for future reference.
   c. Format the disk used to perform the BIOS upgrade.
   d. Set the clear NVRAM jumper on the motherboard.

6. **Joseph was given the task of upgrading the BIOS on his department's NetWare server. During the upgrade, Joseph encountered problems, which caused the server to be down for several hours. What could Joseph have done to prevent this problem? (Choose all that apply.)**
   a. Schedule an appropriate time for the upgrade.
   b. Provide a backup server.
   c. Check the FAQs for the upgrade.
   d. Remove the server from the network.

3.6   Upgrade adapters

PERFORM UPGRADE CHECKLIST

UNDERSTANDING THE OBJECTIVE

Upgrading hardware is a common task for a server technician. When upgrading an adapter, there are several factors that must be taken into consideration to ensure that the upgrade is successful.

WHAT YOU REALLY NEED TO KNOW

◆ You should ensure that the adapter is compatible with your server hardware and software. You may have to upgrade the BIOS on the motherboard to successfully install the adapter. You must also ensure that you have the appropriate **Peripheral Component Interconnect/Industry Standard Architecture (PCI/ISA)** slot for the adapter.

◆ You must know the bus speeds of your PCI slots. Installing a 33 Mhz card in a 66 Mhz PCI slot reduces the speed of the bus to 33 Mhz. This causes bottlenecks and greatly reduces the performance of your server.

◆ Installation of an ISA card almost always requires a configuration (.cfg) file for the device. This file is installed through the EISA Configuration utility. The .cfg file should accompany the drivers for the adapter.

◆ OS vendors publish HCLs that list all devices that are compatible with the OS. HCLs are usually posted on the OS vendor's Web site.

◆ Before starting the installation, you should verify that you have all the necessary software (drivers, firmware, utilities, and so on) to complete the upgrade successfully.

◆ Before installing the adapter, you should ensure that you are properly grounded before handling the adapter. ESD can cause serious damage to components, which can lead to intermittent problems or catastrophic failure of the device.

◆ After the adapter has been installed, you should check the SSU to verify that the system sees the adapter and that no conflicts (IRQs, memory addresses, and so on) exist.

◆ After the server boots, you must install the driver for the adapter. Upon successfully installing the driver, run any updates or patches required by the OS and reboot the server.

◆ After the server boots to the OS, you should verify that the adapter is functioning properly and document the new configuration.

OBJECTIVES ON THE JOB

Organizations are constantly upgrading their servers to increase performance. Upgrading an adapter is a procedure that can be easily accomplished if planned properly. Ensuring compatibility of your server hardware and software greatly increases your chances of performing a successful adapter installation.

PRACTICE TEST QUESTIONS

1. **An ISA adapter normally requires a(n) _____ that is loaded in the _____.**
   a. .icu file, SSU
   b. .cfg file, EISA Configuration utility
   c. .bin file, System Setup utility
   d. .bin file, Registry

2. **Which of the following items must be compatible with an adapter? (Choose all that apply.)**
   a. OS
   b. slot
   c. BIOS
   d. server fan

3. **Adding an adapter may require you to flash the BIOS on the _____.**
   a. memory modules
   b. processor cache
   c. motherboard
   d. Registry

4. **James successfully installed a network card in a Windows NT server. What must James do to enable the operating system to use the network card?**
   a. Attach a network cable to the card.
   b. Upgrade the network card firmware.
   c. Boot the server in Safe Mode.
   d. Add the appropriate driver to the network card.

5. **Todd just finished installing the driver for a network card. Todd should install the required patch _____.**
   a. before rebooting the server
   b. only when the OS asks for the patch
   c. after rebooting the server
   d. when informed by his supervisor

6. **John installed a 33 Mhz PCI adapter in a 66 Mhz slot. Upon rebooting the server, John notices that the server is responding slower than normal. What is causing the problem?**
   a. The BIOS is corrupt.
   b. The Registry needs to be edited.
   c. The adapter slowed down the entire bus.
   d. The driver for the adapter is corrupt.

7. **The IRQ for an adapter can be verified in which of the following ways? (Choose all that apply.)**
   a. in SSU
   b. at POST
   c. during shutdown
   d. in the EISA Configuration Utility

3.7 Upgrade peripheral devices, internal and external

VERIFY APPROPRIATE SYSTEM RESOURCES • PERFORM UPGRADE CHECKLIST

UNDERSTANDING THE OBJECTIVE

Upgrading peripherals is a common procedure for a server technician. You must be able to successfully update internal and external devices for your server.

WHAT YOU REALLY NEED TO KNOW

◆ The device must be compatible with your hardware and software. You should check your hardware and software vendor's compatibility list to verify that the device is compatible.

◆ Before attempting a device upgrade, you should obtain all the necessary documentation for the device that will be installed. Your hardware vendor has additional information for the device. Reading your hardware documentation gives you vital information to assist you with setting up the device.

◆ Always ensure that you have scheduled enough time to properly install the device. Include time to resolve any problems that may occur.

◆ Verify that your server has the necessary resources (slots, IRQs, memory addresses, ports, and so on) to accommodate the new device. Some devices only function if they are set to a specific IRQ or memory address.

◆ You should have all the necessary cables, software, drivers, and mounting hardware for a device before attempting installation. You must also ensure that the device is properly connected after installation.

◆ After you have installed the device, you must verify that the server can see the device. Depending on the type of hardware device installed, there are several ways to verify that the server sees the device. POST, SSU, and SCSI BIOS are excellent tools for determining whether a device was successfully installed.

◆ After verifying that the server sees the device, you must install the appropriate drivers for the device. After the drivers have been successfully installed, the OS should recognize the device.

◆ After the OS has detected the device, you should test the device to ensure that the device is functioning properly.

◆ After you have completed your upgrade process, you should document the changes made to the server and store all the necessary files in a specific location. This ensures that you have the necessary information available if it's required at a future time.

OBJECTIVES ON THE JOB

Sooner or later, you will be asked to perform a peripheral upgrade on a server. By verifying and obtaining all the necessary tools to complete the upgrade successfully, you ensure that your upgrade runs smoothly and is implemented in a timely manner.

PRACTICE TEST QUESTIONS

1. **Ted has been given the task of installing a new external tape backup unit for the organization's file server. Where can Ted acquire documentation and drivers for the device?**
   a. the server vendor's Web site
   b. the OS vendor's Web site
   c. the tape backup vendor's Web site
   d. the network administrator

2. **Which of the following should be checked before installing a hardware device? (Choose all that apply.)**
   a. compatibility
   b. drivers
   c. IRQs
   d. mounting hardware

3. **After you have completely installed a hardware device, what should you do? (Choose all that apply.)**
   a. Reboot the server.
   b. Test the device for functionality.
   c. Check for known issues on the hardware vendor's Web site.
   d. Document the changes for future reference.

4. **HCLs contain which of the following? (Choose all that apply.)**
   a. device model
   b. manufacturer name
   c. product dimensions
   d. supported operating system

5. **Steve is having problems installing a CD-RW drive in his NT server. After two hours of troubleshooting, Steve calls technical support. The technician informs Steve that the drive is not compatible with NT. What could Steve have done to avoid this problem? (Choose all that apply.)**
   a. Steve could have checked the hardware compatibility list (HCL) for NT.
   b. Steve could have contacted the CD-RW vendor for information about the drive.
   c. Steve could have placed the drive on a different cable.
   d. Steve could have read the documentation that was provided with the drive.

6. **James was informed that he should replace the CD-ROM drive in the NetWare server with a faster drive. What should James do first?**
   a. Shut down the server and disconnect the drive.
   b. Schedule an appropriate time to replace the drive.
   c. Unload the CD-ROM module in NetWare.
   d. Disconnect the server from the network.

3.8 Upgrade system monitoring agents

PERFORM UPGRADE CHECKLIST

UNDERSTANDING THE OBJECTIVE

In a networked environment, system monitoring agents receive and relay vital information to technicians about hardware and software. If configured correctly, system monitoring agents can give you information about your network, memory, or even the hard drives in your RAID array.

WHAT YOU REALLY NEED TO KNOW

- ◆ SNMP—This communication protocol monitors and helps manage devices on the network.
- ◆ **Manager**—Polls agents at specified intervals and requests information for the agent. The manager also sets specific variables in the **Management Information Base (MIB)** and the action to occur if a specific condition is met. For example, a parameter could be set to shut down the server if the processor reaches a certain temperature.
- ◆ MIB—An information database that is maintained by the agent.
- ◆ **Agent**—There is a specific agent for each area being monitored. Each agent has a MIB with a specific information set. When a parameter is met or exceeded, the agent sends an SNMP trap to the manager with detailed information about the occurrence that caused the trap to be generated. There can be multiple agents on a single server.
- ◆ System monitoring agents are normally part of a specific monitoring package. Upgrading the software normally consists of running a patch. The patch can be downloaded from the software vendor's Web site. Always verify that you have the correct patch for your OS and version of the software. If upgrading to a newer version of the software, always verify that the newer version gives you the desired results.
- ◆ After completing the upgrade, ensure that your agents are functioning properly. You should also ensure that specific parameters for your agents are configured to their previous settings.

OBJECTIVES ON THE JOB

As a server technician, you will use system monitoring agents to assist you in solving a variety of problems. In a WAN, these agents help you find problems with hardware, networks, and software across multiple segments of the network. Knowing how to configure and upgrade these agents provides you with a wealth of information that assists you with your day-to-day operations.

PRACTICE TEST QUESTIONS

1. The _____ is an information database for an agent.
   a. SIMM
   b. MIB
   c. COS
   d. RTOS

2. SNMP stands for:
   a. Serial Node Multiplier Protocol
   b. Synthetic Network Manager Packet
   c. Signal Node Messaging Packet
   d. Simple Network Management Protocol

3. When a parameter is met or exceeded in the MIB, the agent sends a(n) _____ to the manager.
   a. SNMP trap
   b. pulse
   c. shutdown command
   d. octal code

4. A(n) _____ can set variables in the MIB.
   a. SNMP trap
   b. Manager
   c. node
   d. agent

5. Two weeks ago, Carl updated his system monitoring agents. Today, Carl received several phone calls from users complaining that the network is down. This is the first time Carl has heard of the issue, and he wonders why the network monitoring agent did not notify him of the problem. Carl sees the status of the network segment and there do not appear to be any problems. What would cause the agent not to notify Carl of the issue?
   a. SNMP is not running on the host server.
   b. The parameters in the MIB were set to default when Carl updated the software.
   c. The agent software is corrupt.
   d. The network card in the server is not functioning.

6. Which of the following items can have a system monitoring agent?
   a. processor
   b. server fan
   c. RAID array
   d. all of the above

7. An agent can detect which of the following types of problems? (Choose all that apply.)
   a. network
   b. hardware
   c. upgrade
   d. packet

3.9 Upgrade service tools

PERFORM UPGRADE CHECKLIST

UNDERSTANDING THE OBJECTIVE

Service tools aid technicians in configuring devices and troubleshooting problems when they occur. You must be able to properly upgrade service tools when it is deemed necessary.

WHAT YOU REALLY NEED TO KNOW

◆ Before downloading service tools, you must verify that you have the appropriate tools for your server. Using the wrong service tools can cause you to receive invalid data about your server environment and a host of other problems. You should also check your server vendor's Web site for known issues and FAQs related to your server platform.

◆ You should always maintain the latest service tools for your server. Your server vendor's Web site has specific information about the appropriate tools for your server.

◆ The file for a service tool upgrade can be obtained from your vendor's Web site. The file is normally an executable file that initiates the creation of diskettes when executed or a zipped file that must be extracted and copied to disk.

◆ You should ensure that all your disks are properly labeled upon creation. Your label should contain the utility name, version, and disk number.

◆ After you have successfully created the diskettes for your server, you should test the service tool to ensure that the tool is functioning properly. Testing a service tool usually requires shutting down the server and booting to either a bootable floppy disk or the service tool disk. You should schedule an appropriate time to shut down your server and test your service tools.

◆ Some server manufacturers create a special diagnostic partition on the hard drive that contains multiple service tools for the server. Pressing a specific key combination during POST normally accesses this partition and its utilities. Before attempting to upgrade the diagnostic partition, you should perform a complete backup of the server and verify that the backup was successful. Improperly upgrading the partition can cause the server to experience boot problems. Always thoroughly read the procedures before upgrading a utility partition.

OBJECTIVES ON THE JOB

You will use service tools to assist in resolving many problems. Manufacturers are constantly looking for ways to improve service tools. You should have the most current service tools for every server in your organization. By keeping your service tools up to date, you ensure that you have the necessary tools to configure components and to identify and isolate problems.

PRACTICE TEST QUESTIONS

1. **Sam needs to download the latest EISA Configuration utility for his server. Where can Sam download the necessary file for his server?**
   a. the server vendor's Web site
   b. the OS vendor's Web site
   c. the BIOS vendor's Web site
   d. none of the above

2. **Which of the following are common extensions of downloadable files used to create service tool disks? (Choose all that apply.)**
   a. .bat
   b. .exe
   c. .com
   d. .zip

3. **Diagnostic partitions are located _____.**
   a. on floppy disks
   b. on the server's hard drive
   c. on a CD-ROM
   d. in memory

4. **You should perform a(n) _____ backup before upgrading service tools.**
   a. partial
   b. differential
   c. full
   d. incremental

5. **Which of the following should be checked before downloading a service tool? (Choose all that apply.)**
   a. version
   b. known issues
   c. number of times downloaded
   d. FAQs

6. **Jess has been given the task of upgrading the diagnostics partition on his server. After downloading the file and creating the required disks, what should Jess do?**
   a. Boot the server to the disk he created.
   b. Shut down the server.
   c. Read the documentation that was provided on the disks.
   d. Remove the old diagnostic partition.

7. **The diagnostic partition is normally accessed from which of the following areas?**
   a. within the operating system
   b. across the network
   c. from a special bootable diskette
   d. during POST

3.10 Upgrade UPS

PERFORM UPGRADE CHECKLIST

UNDERSTANDING THE OBJECTIVE

A UPS provides a server with clean and constant AC input. If power is lost, a UPS gives the server the necessary time to shut down. As a server technician, you must be able to successfully upgrade a UPS and its associated software.

WHAT YOU REALLY NEED TO KNOW

- ◆ Ensure that the UPS you select supports the load of all devices that will be attached to it. You must also determine the amount of time that the devices should be available in the event of a power failure.
- ◆ Before installing the UPS, you should check the vendor's Web site for known issues and FAQs.
- ◆ A UPS may come with software that must be configured. Ensure that the software is compatible with your OS before attempting an installation. In addition to the software installation, some operating systems require certain configuration settings. For example, adding the /no serial mice switch to the Boot.ini file of an NT 4.0 server has resolved many problems associated with installing a UPS.
- ◆ Ensure that you have all the proper cables to attach the UPS to the server. Most UPSs use an RS-232 cable and connect to the COM port.
- ◆ Thoroughly inspect the UPS before performing the upgrade. Most companies ship a UPS with the battery disconnected. Check to ensure that all cables are connected. You may be required to charge the UPS battery before putting it into operation.
- ◆ The UPS must be verified and configured by your operating system. If the UPS is configured incorrectly, it prematurely shuts down the server.
- ◆ After you have completed the upgrade, verify that the UPS, operating system, and software are functioning properly, and then document your configuration for future reference.

OBJECTIVES ON THE JOB

A UPS is a valuable part of your overall configuration. When upgrading your UPS, be certain that you have looked at all the necessary steps to ensure that your upgrade runs smoothly. By carefully planning the installation and choosing the appropriate hardware and software to meet your organization's needs, you can prevent problems that are commonly associated with installation.

PRACTICE TEST QUESTIONS

1. **Which of the following is important when upgrading a UPS?**
   - a. power load
   - b. inspecting the UPS
   - c. OS compatibility
   - d. all of the above

2. **Jack is upgrading the UPS installed in his server rack. The rack has four servers, two external tape backup units, a keyboard, and two monitors. Which items should Jack include in determining the total power needed for his new UPS? (Choose all that apply.)**
   - a. the four servers
   - b. the two monitors
   - c. the keyboard
   - d. the tape backup units

3. **What type of cable is used to connect the UPS to the server?**
   - a. Centronics 50-pin
   - b. DB-25 connector
   - c. RS-232 cable
   - d. RS-323 cable

4. **A UPS can help mitigate the effects of which of the following problems?**
   - a. power surges
   - b. spikes
   - c. brownouts
   - d. all of the above

5. **Jennifer just received a new UPS from shipping. After unpacking the UPS, she plugs in the device and discovers that none of the lights on the front of the UPS are illuminating. She changes power outlets and receives the same results. What is most likely the problem?**
   - a. The outlet is not supplying enough voltage.
   - b. The power cord is bad.
   - c. The UPS battery is disconnected.
   - d. The UPS was damaged during shipping.

6. **Larry is having problems installing his UPS. When the UPS is attached to the server, the UPS starts to beep and shuts down the server automatically. Larry believes that there may be an answer to the problem on the Web. Whose Web site should Larry search for the solution?**
   - a. the server vendor's Web site
   - b. the OS vendor's Web site
   - c. the UPS vendor's Web site
   - d. all of the above

7. **Which of the following should be performed after installing a UPS?**
   - a. Configure the UPS in the OS.
   - b. Document the configuration.
   - c. Install UPS software.
   - d. all of the above

4.1   Perform regular backup

PERFORM REGULAR BACKUP

UNDERSTANDING THE OBJECTIVE

Performing backups is one of the most important procedures you will perform. Backups ensure data recovery in the event of a catastrophic server problem. As a server technician, you must be aware of the different types of backups and their recovery procedures.

WHAT YOU REALLY NEED TO KNOW

◆ You must understand the following types of backups:

- *Full backup*—Backs up everything (files and directories) on the server. Some companies perform more than one full backup per week; you should perform one full backup per week at a minimum.

- *Incremental backup*—Backs up all files that have changed since the last backup. If you had to restore a server using incremental backups, you would first restore the full backup, and then restore all the incrementals to ensure all data was recovered.

- *Differential backup*—Backs up all files since the last full backup. If you had to restore a server using a differential backup, you could restore the server with only two backup sets.

◆ Regardless of the type of backup you perform, always verify that the data successfully backed up to tape. Problems verifying a tape could indicate a problem with your tape, tape drive, or verification software.

◆ You should regularly rotate your tapes. This prolongs the life of your tapes and prevents future problems. Receiving errors (in one or multiple locations) on a tape could be an indication that the tape is bad.

◆ You should clean your tape drive regularly. Many tape backup issues have been resolved by properly cleaning the tape backup unit. Your hardware vendor should have additional information on the frequency for cleaning your tape backup unit.

◆ You will encounter backup software that is native to your OS as well as third-party software. You should research all information (FAQs, updates, and so on) for the software. Some third-party software even requires a different driver for the tape backup unit to function correctly. Your software vendor's Web site should have information for your specific product.

◆ Always ensure that your tapes are properly labeled. Proper labeling ensures that your tapes remain with their correct set and prevents mixing of your backup sets.

OBJECTIVES ON THE JOB

Performing routine backups ensures recovery when a server crashes and must be restored. When an organization loses data, the cost of recovering it can be significant. Many technicians are no longer technicians because they failed to perform routine backups. Consider the different backup types, and ensure that the routine backup procedure you choose meets your organization's needs.

PRACTICE TEST QUESTIONS

1. **Kira ran a full backup on Friday and incremental backups on Monday through Wednesday. If the server crashes on Thursday, how many backup sets does Kira need to recover the server?**
   a. one
   b. two
   c. four
   d. six

2. **What does a full backup back up?**
   a. all files and directories
   b. volumes
   c. batch files only
   d. executable files only

3. **Joe received an error while verifying a tape. Joe restarts the verification process and the job fails again at the same location on the tape. What caused the verification to fail?**
   a. The tape backup unit needs to be cleaned.
   b. The backup tape is bad.
   c. The software used to verify the backup needs to be reinstalled.
   d. The driver for the tape backup unit is corrupt.

4. **An incremental backup:**
   a. backs up all files that have changed since the last full backup
   b. backs up all files
   c. backs up all files that have changed since the last backup
   d. backs up only the files you select

5. **Stewart performed a full backup of the server on Saturday and differential backups on Monday through Thursday. If the server crashes on Friday, how many backup sets does Stewart need to restore the server?**
   a. two
   b. three
   c. four
   d. five

6. **Which of the following are important when performing routine backups? (Choose all that apply.)**
   a. a clean tape backup unit
   b. verification of the backup
   c. bytes per second transferred to the tape
   d. proper labeling of the tape

7. **After restoring a server using backup sets, John realizes that the data on the server is incorrect. John discovers that he restored the server using an incremental and differential backup. How could John have prevented this problem?**
   a. Store differential backups offsite.
   b. Store incremental backups offsite.
   c. Place different backup sets in separate cabinets.
   d. Properly label the backup sets.

4.2 Create baseline and compare performance

CREATE BASELINE AND COMPARE PERFORMANCE

UNDERSTANDING THE OBJECTIVE

Server baselines are used to analyze system performance. Baselines can be run to determine performance on everything from server hardware to network activity. Baselines are very useful tools for troubleshooting and upgrades.

WHAT YOU REALLY NEED TO KNOW

- ◆ There are third-party software utilities available for performing server **baselines**, but most OSs have native utilities that can be configured to perform a server baseline.

- ◆ When establishing a server baseline, you should first determine what activities should be measured. You should measure the following activities: server utilization, memory usage, disk utilization, and processor utilization. Measuring these system components provides you with information about your server's performance.

- ◆ A baseline should be performed on a new server when it is integrated into the network. The information from this baseline gives you a **benchmark** for the server. Future baselines can be compared to this baseline to ensure the server is performing at the desired level.

- ◆ You should perform a baseline during peak operations. This baseline identifies bottlenecks and provides you with the necessary information to determine which server components should be upgraded.

- ◆ View the information from your baseline thoroughly. High percentages of utilization can identify hardware problems and software configuration issues.

- ◆ Before attempting to upgrade server hardware, you should check that your OS is configured correctly. Many bottlenecks can be resolved by optimizing settings in your OS. For example, creating a larger paging file or moving the paging file across multiple drives may resolve problems with memory. Your software vendor has additional information to assist you with optimization.

- ◆ If a hardware upgrade is required, a baseline should be performed after the upgrade to ensure that desired results were obtained.

OBJECTIVES ON THE JOB

As an organization grows, so does the amount of users, files, applications, and activity across the network. Degradation in performance and slow network access are usually indications that a configuration or hardware upgrade is required. Server baselines provide you with the necessary information to determine what problems exist across your network and to configure your server for optimal performance.

PRACTICE TEST QUESTIONS

1. **After performing a server baseline, you discover that memory utilization and disk utilization percentages are very high. Which of the following actions could possibly resolve the problem? (Choose all that apply.)**
   - a. Upgrade RAM.
   - b. Upgrade the processor.
   - c. Upgrade hard drives.
   - d. Optimize memory in the OS.

2. **Which of the following activities should you consider measuring when performing a server baseline? (Choose all that apply.)**
   - a. disk utilization
   - b. server utilization
   - c. processor utilization
   - d. memory usage

3. **When should you perform a server baseline?**
   - a. just before users arrive at work
   - b. during peak network activity
   - c. during lunch
   - d. when all users have logged off the network

4. **Performing a baseline on a new server can:**
   - a. provide a benchmark for the server
   - b. slow network performance
   - c. corrupt the Registry
   - d. remove outdated files

5. **Chris performed three server baselines during the week. The % Processor Time for all three baselines was at 93%. What should Chris do?**
   - a. Upgrade the RAM.
   - b. Upgrade the hard drives.
   - c. Upgrade the processor.
   - d. Upgrade the motherboard.

6. **While performing a server baseline, you discover your % Disk Time is consistently at 95%. What should you do?**
   - a. Replace the hard drive(s).
   - b. Add RAM.
   - c. Replace the processor.
   - d. Patch the server.

7. **When is the best time to perform a server baseline?**
   - a. when users are arriving for work
   - b. during lunch
   - c. midday
   - d. when users are logged off the server

4.3   Set SNMP thresholds

SET SNMP THRESHOLDS

UNDERSTANDING THE OBJECTIVE

SNMP eases the task of network management. After SNMP thresholds are properly configured, a technician can receive vital information and alerts about hardware, software, and network activity.

WHAT YOU REALLY NEED TO KNOW

◆ **Thresholds** are set using network management software. The threshold variable is set for a specific object. The variable is stored in a MIB and monitored by the agent.

◆ To set a threshold level for a device, an agent for the device must be present. An agent has information about a device and that information is stored in a MIB.

◆ To monitor activity and set specific thresholds for a device, familiarize yourself with various network management systems that work with SNMP. You should check your management software vendor's Web site for FAQs, updates, and known issues.

◆ Never set an SNMP threshold without verifying that the setting is correct for the device. If a threshold setting is too high, an alert will not be generated and you will not receive vital server information. If a threshold setting is too low, you may receive constant messages on a device that is functioning properly.

◆ When setting SNMP threshold levels, you must also set the interval at which the agent polls the device for information. Be certain that the interval you set for the device is correct. Constant polling of a device can cause network performance problems.

◆ The agent generates an **SNMP trap** when a device reaches a certain set condition. For example, if a processor is set to send an alert when the temperature reaches 150 degrees, the agent sends an SNMP trap to the management station when the condition is met. Other actions, such as automatically shutting down the server and notifying the system administrator, also can be specified.

◆ When updating your management software, you should record your threshold settings before performing the update. After the update is complete, you should verify that all of your settings are correct and that your software functions properly.

OBJECTIVES ON THE JOB

Setting SNMP thresholds can greatly reduce the amount of time spent troubleshooting a problem and provide you with valuable information about your server. You can use management software to check the health of a RAID array, monitor the RPMs of your server fans, or see exactly which memory module is causing problems in your server and in which slot it is located. You should consider the benefits of using management software within your organization and the thresholds that can be set to effectively manage your server environment.

PRACTICE TEST QUESTIONS

1. **SNMP thresholds are set using _____.**
   a. interpreter strings
   b. MIB utility
   c. management software
   d. SNMP traps

2. **When a threshold variable is set, the information is stored in the _____.**
   a. MIB
   b. DIMM
   c. IBM
   d. graphical database

3. **Barbara just set the threshold level for the processor temperature to send an alert if the processor reaches 150 degrees. Barbara also set the polling interval to poll the device every five seconds. After making the changes, Barbara notices that the network is very slow. What should Barbara do to resolve the problem?**
   a. Add additional RAM.
   b. Increase the polling interval.
   c. Defrag the hard drives.
   d. Decrease the polling interval.

4. **Constant polling of a managed device will:**
   a. increase network performance
   b. slow network performance
   c. generate an SNMP trap
   d. none of the above

5. **A threshold level that is set too high will _____.**
   a. send a constant alert to the management station
   b. automatically shut down the server
   c. not inform the system administrator of a vital error
   d. corrupt the MIB

6. **The _____ monitors a specific device and sends an SNMP trap to the _____ when a specified condition is met.**
   a. MIB, agent
   b. agent, management station
   c. variable, MIB
   d. management station, agent

7. **In order to store information about a device, a(n) _____ must be present for the device.**
   a. MIB
   b. trap
   c. monitor
   d. agent

4.4   Perform physical housekeeping

PERFORM PHYSICAL HOUSEKEEPING

UNDERSTANDING THE OBJECTIVE

Physical housekeeping is an important aspect of proactive maintenance. Routine housekeeping procedures reduce problems that contribute to premature failures and equipment loss.

WHAT YOU REALLY NEED TO KNOW

◆ You should always maintain a clean server environment. Dust and debris in the server area can cause major problems. Servers have a constant flow of air circulating through the chassis to ensure cooling. Dust can restrict airflow and cause components to overheat.

◆ A preventive maintenance schedule should be established to ensure that your servers are cleaned on a regular basis. Proper cleanings extend server life and reduce failure of components.

◆ Internal server components should be cleaned with low-pressure air.

◆ Ensure that your monitors, keyboards, and mice are cleaned on a regular basis. Proper cleaning can prevent problems (stuck keys, poor mouse movement, and so on) with these devices.

◆ All tools should be labeled and placed in a specific location. This prevents you from having to search for a specific tool or purchase another tool to replace a missing one. Some tools can cost hundreds of dollars to replace.

◆ Items should be removed from the floor and stored in their respective locations. Excess items (power cords, books, tools, and equipment) can clutter a work area and make it difficult to find an item that is required to perform your job. Leaving items scattered in your environment is also a safety hazard and could cause someone to trip and sustain injuries.

◆ All electrical components (for example, cards, adapters, and printed circuit boards) should be enclosed in their protective packaging and stored in their respective locations. ESD can cause damage to components and cause them to fail during operation.

◆ Keep food and beverages out of your server area. Spilling coffee into a server can cost a company a considerable amount of money—equipment may need to be replaced. If beverages are allowed in your area, guidelines should be set to determine the appropriate type of container (for instance, spill-proof).

OBJECTIVES ON THE JOB

Proactive maintenance consists of solving a problem before it becomes a problem. Regular inspections and cleanings can prolong the life of your server and all associated components. Physical housekeeping enhances productivity, safety, and asset management in your server environment.

PRACTICE TEST QUESTIONS

1. **Which of the following items are considered part of performing physical housekeeping? (Choose all that apply.)**
   a. cleaning a PCB with a cloth
   b. moving a container of coffee away from the server
   c. performing regular inspections
   d. sweeping and mopping the server room

2. **Which of the following are threats to a server environment? (Choose all that apply.)**
   a. dust and debris
   b. an uncovered coffee container
   c. power cords lying on the floor
   d. a frayed power cord

3. **Xavier has been given the task of replacing a network card at a customer's site. Upon opening the chassis, Xavier discovers that the server's components are very dusty. What should Xavier do?**
   a. Clean the server with low-pressure air.
   b. Clean the components with a damp cloth.
   c. Use gloves when installing the network card.
   d. Clean the server with a cloth or brush.

4. **Which of the following is not a form of physical housekeeping?**
   a. cleaning keyboards and mice
   b. leaving tools scattered on a workbench
   c. restricting food from the server room
   d. changing air filters in the server room

5. **Carla upgraded four of her company's eight database servers. She has just completed the last server. What should she do next? (Choose all that apply.)**
   a. Leave her tools on the workbench and go home.
   b. Return all unused components to their proper location.
   c. Leave components on the workbench.
   d. Return all tools to the toolbox.

6. **Which of the following can occur if there are excessive amounts of dust in a server? (Choose all that apply.)**
   a. The server may overheat.
   b. The system may crash.
   c. There may be chassis damage.
   d. There may be intermittent failures.

7. **Server components should be cleaned with which of the following?**
   a. cloth
   b. brush
   c. anti-static spray
   d. low-pressure air

4.5   Perform hardware verification

PERFORM HARDWARE VERIFICATION

UNDERSTANDING THE OBJECTIVE

Servers have many different types of hardware (hard drives, network cards, memory, and so on) installed. Hardware verification is an important aspect of server maintenance and it enables you to quickly replace and configure defective hardware when problems arise.

WHAT YOU REALLY NEED TO KNOW

- ◆ The more information you have about the hardware in your server, the easier it is to maintain the server. When verifying your server hardware, you should ask yourself the following questions:
    1. In which server does the hardware reside?
    2. What type of hardware (for example, CD-ROM, RAID controller, tape backup unit) is it?
    3. Who is the manufacturer of the hardware?
    4. What is the model number of the hardware?
    5. What is the serial number of the hardware?
    6. In what slot does the hardware reside?
    7. What IRQs, IDs, and memory addresses are the devices using?
    8. What drivers are used with the hardware?
    9. What is the BIOS/firmware revision level of the hardware?
    10. What are the specific settings (hardware and software) for the device?

- ◆ After you have obtained all the required information about your hardware configuration, you should document the information and maintain a hard copy and soft copy for every server within your organization. You also should store a copy of your hardware configuration off site for future reference.

- ◆ Properly documented hardware configurations allow hardware replacement to be performed efficiently and with fewer problems.

- ◆ When replacing or upgrading hardware, document the changes. This makes your information current and prevents problems with future hardware replacements.

OBJECTIVES ON THE JOB

Unless all of your servers are identical, your hardware configurations will vary from server to server. Hardware verification ensures that when you do have to replace a device, it is replaced with the correct device, thus saving a considerable amount of time. You will encounter many different server platforms as a server technician. You should familiarize yourself with those platforms and the hardware that resides in them.

PRACTICE TEST QUESTIONS

1. **Nicole has been given the task of gathering information about the NICs located in the company's three application servers. What information should Nicole include in her documentation? (Choose all that apply.)**
   a. type of NIC
   b. manufacturer
   c. status lights
   d. NIC IRQ

2. **After performing hardware verification procedures, what should you do? (Choose all that apply.)**
   a. Document the information.
   b. Update your information when changes occur.
   c. Create a hard copy and a soft copy of the information.
   d. Store the documentation in a notebook in the server room.

3. **Which of the following are good places to store hardware verification documentation? (Choose all that apply.)**
   a. an Excel spreadsheet on the file server
   b. the library in the system administrator's office
   c. a notebook
   d. off site in hard copy format

4. **Which of the following should be documented when performing hardware verification?**
   a. hardware configurations
   b. software configurations
   c. drivers
   d. all of the above

5. **Lawrence received a shipment of new hard drives. What information should Lawrence document to assist with hardware verification? (Choose all that apply.)**
   a. manufacturer
   b. number of pins on the drive
   c. model of the drive
   d. hard drive size

6. **What can hardware verification do? (Choose all that apply.)**
   a. greatly assist with disaster recovery
   b. increase the amount of time it takes to configure a device
   c. ensure that you have the correct replacement hardware
   d. cost you more time than it's worth

7. **Jameson just updated the RAID controller firmware on the server. Which documentation should Jameson update?**
   a. hard copy
   b. soft copy
   c. offsite
   d. all of the above

4.6   Establish remote notification

ESTABLISH REMOTE NOTIFICATION

UNDERSTANDING THE OBJECTIVE

Most organizations have multiple servers in multiple locations. Server technicians are responsible for maintaining those servers and ensuring that they are online and available at all times. Remote notification is the first step to providing quick response time to an issue.

WHAT YOU REALLY NEED TO KNOW

- ◆ Remote notification provides a technician with vital information about system processes, failures, and alerts. Failed drives in RAID arrays, downed servers, and network segments are all critical factors in a server environment.

- ◆ Remote notification is normally handled by network management software. The methods of remote notification vary with software packages, but most packages provide you with a set of common features. You should check your network management software vendor's documentation or Web site for specific information on your software package.

- ◆ Most network management software allows you to set remote notification options when configuring SNMP threshold options. When the specific condition of the object is met, the agent sends an SNMP trap to the management station and a technician is notified of the incident.

- ◆ After configuring remote notification, always test your configuration to ensure connectivity and document the changes to the server's configuration.

- ◆ The most common methods of remote notification are as follows:

  Paging—When the server receives an alert with a specific condition, remote notification software automatically dials a number to inform a technician. The server has a dedicated modem for paging. If you are constantly in the field or away from your work area, the paging option is a resourceful tool.

  E-mail—When the server receives an alert, the software sends the alert to a specific e-mail address. When using this method, make sure multiple people receive the e-mail notification. For example, instead of sending the notification message to bob@yourcompany.com, send the message to administrators@yourcompany.com. This ensures that everyone in the Administration Department receives the message, including Bob, who may be out to lunch or on vacation.

OBJECTIVES ON THE JOB

As a technician, you will be exposed to multiple ways to establish remote notification. Remote notification reduces the amount of downtime associated with server problems and warns server technicians about potential problems. You should consider the different possibilities when establishing a remote notification process for your organization.

PRACTICE TEST QUESTIONS

1. **Remote notification can send messages for which of the following alerts? (Choose all that apply.)**
   a. bad network card
   b. downed server
   c. failed hard drive
   d. excessive page faults

2. **Remote notification is normally handled by the _____.**
   a. MIB
   b. hard drive
   c. network management software
   d. hierarchal database

3. **Barry is configuring his network management software to send an alert message to an e-mail address. Which of the following would be the best address to use?**
   a. barryj@hiscompany.com
   b. sysadmin@hiscompany.com
   c. barryM@hiscompany.com
   d. frankC@hiscompany.com

4. **Which of the following play a major role in remote notification? (Choose all that apply.)**
   a. management software
   b. SNMP
   c. agents
   d. networks

5. **Carlton has just set up remote notification for his server. What should Carlton do next? (Choose all that apply.)**
   a. Test his remote notification settings.
   b. Update the MIB.
   c. Document the new settings.
   d. Do nothing.

6. **Sam discovered that a drive in his RAID 5 array has failed. Sam had configured the network management software to page him in the event of a drive failure. He did not receive a page. Which items should Sam check when troubleshooting the issue? (Choose all that apply.)**
   a. the SNMP threshold setting for the array
   b. the pager number entered
   c. the system power supply
   d. the modem

7. **Fran needs a patch for her network management software. Whom should she contact for information about the required patch?**
   a. operating system vendor
   b. server vendor
   c. management software vendor
   d. none of the above

5.1   Recognize and report on physical security issues

LIMIT ACCESS TO SERVER ROOM AND BACKUP TAPES • ENSURE PHYSICAL LOCKS EXIST ON DOORS • ESTABLISH ANTI-THEFT DEVICES FOR HARDWARE (LOCK SERVER RACKS)

UNDERSTANDING THE OBJECTIVE

Limiting access to your servers and associated hardware is an important aspect of physical security. You must be able to identify, report, and resolve physical security issues.

WHAT YOU REALLY NEED TO KNOW

◆ All entrances to the server room should have locks installed to prevent unauthorized access. All keys to the server room should be numbered and their locations documented to ensure that all keys are accounted for. Some organizations use cyper locks to control access to the server room. **Cyper locks** have a keypad that is programmed with a specific combination of numbers. When the correct combination is entered, the person is granted access to the server room.

◆ Only authorized personnel (such as technicians, administrators, and analysts) should have access to the server room. There should not be a constant flow of user traffic in the server room. If an unauthorized person must enter the server room, he or she should be escorted at all times.

◆ You must ensure that your server hardware is secure at all times. Server manufacturers have integrated locks into the server chassis to prevent the server's cover and hard drives from being removed. If your servers are rack-mounted, you must also ensure that your server racks are locked.

◆ Backups contain valuable information about an organization's business. If that information were to fall into the hands of a malicious person, the results could severely damage an organization. All backup tapes should be properly secured to limit access. You should maintain documentation of your backup tapes and take an inventory of them on a regular basis.

◆ Before leaving the office, you should ensure that all doors are locked and that all hardware has been secured in its appropriate location. Establishing checklists can greatly assist you in verifying that all tasks are completed.

◆ It is very important to perform regular inspections of the server room. Inspections help identify problems with security. When a discrepancy is discovered, it should be reported immediately. Most organizations have a standard procedure for reporting discrepancies. You must familiarize yourself with your organization's policy for handling and reporting security issues.

OBJECTIVES ON THE JOB

Security is a responsibility of all personnel at an organization. You must ensure that measures are in place to protect your server and other assets. You should consider ways of enhancing security within your organization and perform regular inspections to ensure that set standards are enforced.

PRACTICE TEST QUESTIONS

1. **Mashone is performing a security inspection of the server room. Which of the following items should Mashone include in her report? (Choose all that apply.)**
   a. unlocked server rack
   b. tools left on the workbench
   c. unlocked server room doors
   d. coffee on the computer desk

2. **Who should have access to the server room? (Choose all that apply.)**
   a. technicians
   b. systems analysts
   c. users
   d. system administrators

3. **An A/C repairman must perform scheduled maintenance in the server room. What should you do?**
   a. Take the repairman to the server room and leave him to complete his work.
   b. Give the repairman the combination to the cyper lock.
   c. Escort the repairman to the server room. Remain with the repairman.
   d. Instruct the repairman to come back later.

4. **James received a report that a server room door was left unlocked overnight. The technicians should secure all doors and perform other tasks before leaving the building for the day. What should he do to ensure all doors are secured and all tasks are completed?**
   a. Check all doors before leaving the building.
   b. Send a memo to his manager.
   c. Establish a checklist of all tasks to be performed.
   d. Inform technicians during the next meeting.

5. **What should be done to protect the information contained on backup tapes? (Choose all that apply.)**
   a. Properly secure all backup tapes to limit access.
   b. Maintain documentation of backup tapes.
   c. Take an inventory of backup tapes on a regular basis.
   d. Store the copy of the backup tape in the server room.

6. **During a walk-through inspection, John discovers that the room where the hubs and routers are located does not have a lock installed on the door. What should John do? (Choose all that apply.)**
   a. Document the discrepancy.
   b. Do nothing.
   c. Report the issue to the appropriate person(s).
   d. Block the door with a heavy object.

7. **Which of the following should have locks installed to prevent unauthorized access?**
   a. server room doors
   b. tape cabinets
   c. server racks
   d. all of the above

5.2   Recognize and report on server room environmental issues

RECOGNIZE AND REPORT ON SERVER ROOM ENVIRONMENTAL ISSUES

UNDERSTANDING THE OBJECTIVE

Your server environment plays a key role in the vitality of your servers. You must be able to identify environmental threats and establish methods that reduce their likelihood.

WHAT YOU REALLY NEED TO KNOW

◆ Temperature and humidity can wreak havoc on a server environment. Servers are designed to function at a specific temperature. If that temperature is exceeded, a server can experience serious problems. You should always ensure that your server environment meets the requirements of your servers. It is important to monitor the temperature and humidity at all times. Most organizations have a monitoring device that alerts personnel when temperature and humidity limits are exceeded. Ensuring that your A/C equipment is sufficient for your environment assists you in minimizing the threat of temperature and humidity.

◆ ESD can cause serious damage to components and contribute to increased downtime and repair. Ensuring that workstations are grounded and training personnel on ESD procedures greatly assist you in combating ESD. Wrist straps, sprays, and ionizers are just a few of the tools that can be used to help decrease issues that are related to ESD.

◆ Power is very important to a server environment. Power surges, spikes, and brownouts can cause serious damage to equipment. Surge protectors and UPSs can be used to prevent damage caused by power issues. Some organizations must remain operational in the event of a power outage. A UPS gives you a small amount of time, normally enough for your servers to shut down gracefully. Backup generators can provide you with enough power to remain operational for extended periods of time.

◆ Fire is a threat that no one wants to encounter, but it must be prepared for. Be familiar with the operation of the fire suppression system installed in your server room. Know where the fire extinguishers are located and how to operate them. There are different fire extinguishers for different classes of fires. You should ensure that you have the correct extinguisher for your environment.

◆ Flooding is another threat for which you must be prepared. Water damage can be the death of a server. You should ensure that your servers are placed in a location that reduces the likelihood of damage caused by flooding.

◆ Your server environment should be monitored and the results documented to ensure that your environment remains within the specified standards.

OBJECTIVES ON THE JOB

A carefully planned server environment reduces the possibility of threats that can cripple an organization. You should always be aware of your server environment and constantly seek methods to improve it.

PRACTICE TEST QUESTIONS

1. **Terry needs to ensure that his servers will remain operational during a power outage. Which of the following is the best choice for Terry's servers?**
   - a. UPS
   - b. surge protector
   - c. power strip
   - d. backup generator

2. **Which of the following can cause problems in a server environment? (Choose all that apply.)**
   - a. power surges
   - b. humidity
   - c. water
   - d. fire

3. **Which of the following can reduce the likelihood of ESD damage? (Choose all that apply.)**
   - a. trained personnel
   - b. ionizers
   - c. wrist straps
   - d. power cords

4. **Which of the following is the best area to place a server in a server room?**
   - a. on the floor
   - b. near a window
   - c. in a cabinet or rack
   - d. none of the above

5. **Which of the following protects a server against a power surge? (Choose all that apply.)**
   - a. grounded outlet
   - b. surge protector
   - c. UPS
   - d. power cord

6. **Information about the maximum operating temperature of a server can be obtained from which of the following?**
   - a. system BIOS
   - b. server vendor
   - c. software vendor
   - d. none of the above

7. **Paul installed a new Windows NT server in his department. The server is plugged into a surge protector, and the surge protector is plugged into a UPS. If a power outage occurs, the server will:**
   - a. power off immediately
   - b. gracefully shutdown after several minutes
   - c. run for several hours
   - d. none of the above

6.1   Perform problem determination

USE QUESTIONING TECHNIQUES TO DETERMINE WHAT, HOW, WHEN • IDENTIFY CONTACT(S) RESPONSIBLE FOR PROBLEM RESOLUTION • USE SENSES TO OBSERVE PROBLEM

UNDERSTANDING THE OBJECTIVE

When troubleshooting an issue, there may be many possible causes of the problem. A server technician must be able to determine the root cause and provide the resolution.

WHAT YOU REALLY NEED TO KNOW

◆ Before troubleshooting an issue, you should always verify the customer's name, organization, address, and telephone number. Never assume a customer's information is valid. People move into other positions, and organizations move into bigger and better locations. Failure to verify customer information can cause technicians and parts to be sent to the wrong location and other service delays. If possible, get a second contact in case your primary contact is unavailable when service arrives.

◆ Before taking steps to resolve an issue, you must determine the origin of the problem. Using effective questioning procedures assists you in identifying and isolating a problem. Asking the following questions can provide you with the necessary information to successfully determine the cause of the problem:

- *When* did the problem occur?

- *How* many users are unable to log on?

- *What* error message did you receive?

- *What* OS is the server running?

◆ When a situation involves going to a customer's physical location to resolve a problem, you first should perform a thorough observation of the server and its environment. Are all cables, power cords, and devices properly connected? Is there a smell of smoke in the room? If so, can you determine where the smell is coming from? What is the temperature of the server environment? Is the server room clean or filled with dust and debris? Information from your observations may help you to discover a much larger problem than imagined or prevent you from spending a considerable amount of time troubleshooting an issue that could have been resolved by tightening a loose cable.

OBJECTIVES ON THE JOB

Technicians resolve many issues using effective questioning and observation procedures. Mastering these skills greatly enhances your troubleshooting abilities and provides your customers with accurate and timely service. You should always remember that when a customer's server is down, it can cost the company a considerable amount of money. You should consider how using effective questioning can save your organization time and money.

PRACTICE TEST QUESTIONS

1. **Jason just received a call from a customer about a server issue. What information should Jason ask for? (Choose all that apply.)**
   a. the customer's organization
   b. the customer's name
   c. the customer's telephone number
   d. the customer's address

2. **Upon arriving onsite, Mashone was informed that users are unable to log on to the network. What questions should Mashone ask the customer? (Choose all that apply.)**
   a. When did the problem start?
   b. What errors are you receiving?
   c. Can anyone log on to the network?
   d. What type of hard drive is installed?

3. **Frank has been called onsite to repair a server that will not power on. What procedure should Frank perform first?**
   a. Remove and reseat all cards inside the server.
   b. Replace the power supply.
   c. Restart the UPS attached to the server.
   d. Inspect the server to ensure that all cables and cords are connected.

4. **Albert has just been called onsite to replace a failed hard drive. Upon entering the server room, Albert notices that the room is very humid. What should Albert do?**
   a. Replace the hard drive and inform the customer about the humidity.
   b. Do nothing.
   c. Replace the hard drive.
   d. Power down all servers and inform the customer of the humidity problem.

5. **Mary received a call from a very upset customer. The customer has been waiting for a technician who is two hours late. Upon researching the issue, Mary discovers the technician was sent to the wrong address. How could this problem have been avoided? (Choose all that apply.)**
   a. Verify the customer's information before sending a technician.
   b. Mary should have gone on the call herself.
   c. Select a technician in the customer's area.
   d. Update the customer's information in the system.

6. **Jasmine has been given the task of replacing the motherboard on a server. Upon opening the server chassis, Jasmine smells an odor inside the server. What should Jasmine do?**
   a. Inspect the server to determine the origin of the smell.
   b. Replace the motherboard and leave the site.
   c. Inform the customer that she cannot replace the motherboard.
   d. none of the above

6.2 Use diagnostic hardware and software tools and utilities

IDENTIFY COMMON DIAGNOSTIC TOOLS ACROSS THE FOLLOWING OPERATING SYSTEMS: WINDOWS NT/2000 • USE THE SELECTED TOOL EFFECTIVELY

UNDERSTANDING THE OBJECTIVE

Windows NT/2000 has native diagnostic utilities to assist in problem identification and resolution. This section discusses the tools and utilities available in Windows NT/2000.

WHAT YOU REALLY NEED TO KNOW

- ◆ *Event Viewer*—Displays application, system, and security logs. This information is essential to troubleshoot issues. Use the Event Viewer logs to determine what failed and why. For example, a Windows service that depends on another service to start may fail if that service fails to start. The Event Viewer gives you the information on the failed service as well as the service that caused the failure.

- ◆ *Performance Monitor/Tool*—Enables you to track system performance by enabling specific counters for an object. Objects monitored can be hardware (memory, hard drives, and processor) and software processes. Information from this utility can identify system bottlenecks and provide the data necessary to isolate and identify the problem. Information from this utility can become a server baseline.

- ◆ *Task Manager*—Displays information about applications and processes running on the server. The Applications tab displays all tasks running and their status. An application that is not responding can be terminated. The Processes tab displays all processes running on the server. Also displayed are **packet identifiers (PIDs)**, CPU usage, time, and memory usage. You can end a process that is taking up a considerable amount of system resources. The Performance tab provides a graphic display of usage and history for the CPU and memory as well as detailed information about memory.

- ◆ *Network Monitor*—Displays information on network utilization and packets. This utility is a very useful tool for monitoring network activity and troubleshooting network problems.

- ◆ *Commands:*
  - *winmsd*—Displays valuable information on system, hardware, and software environments.
  - *ipconfig/all*—Displays all the IP settings for the network adapter(s) installed in the server.
  - *ping*—Verifies connectivity between devices on a TCP/IP network.

- ◆ Using the selected tool effectively reduces the time required to diagnose an issue.

OBJECTIVES ON THE JOB

Learning the proper use of Windows NT/2000 diagnostic utilities helps to diagnose server problems and keep networks running smoothly.

PRACTICE TEST QUESTIONS

1. **Steve has been given the task of verifying how much memory his NT server is using. What utility should Steve use to accomplish this? (Choose all that apply.)**
   a. Event Viewer
   b. winmsd
   c. Task Manager
   d. Network Manager

2. **The _____ can be used to display application, system, and security logs.**
   a. Registry Editor
   b. Task Manager
   c. Event Viewer
   d. Hierarchical Database

3. **The _____ can be used to end an application that is not responding.**
   a. Registry Editor
   b. Task Manager
   c. Event Viewer
   d. Network Monitor

4. **Which of the following can be used to verify connectivity between devices on a TCP/IP network?**
   a. ipsec
   b. ping
   c. RCONSOLE
   d. ipconfig

5. **Xavier needs to verify the IP addresses for all network cards in the server. Which utility can Xavier use to accomplish this?**
   a. Ipsec
   b. Ipconfig
   c. Winmsd
   d. Tracer

6. **Shelly received an error during startup that a service failed to start. Where could Shelly view information about the error?**
   a. winmsd
   b. Event Viewer
   c. Performance Monitor
   d. Task Manager

7. **The _____ can be used to display information about network utilization, activity, and packets.**
   a. Performance Monitor
   b. Network Monitor
   c. Registry Editor
   d. Task Manager

6.2   Use diagnostic hardware and software tools and utilities (continued)

IDENTIFY COMMON DIAGNOSTIC TOOLS ACROSS THE FOLLOWING OPERATING SYSTEMS: NOVELL NETWARE • SELECT THE APPROPRIATE TOOL

UNDERSTANDING THE OBJECTIVE

When hardware problems or performance issues occur on your NetWare server, you must be able to diagnose and resolve the problem. NetWare provides numerous console tools to perform diagnostics. Selecting the correct tool is key to your success.

WHAT YOU REALLY NEED TO KNOW

◆ Commands are run from the console prompt. Pressing Alt+Esc takes you to the console prompt. Be familiar with the following diagnostic utilities and their uses in a NetWare environment:

◆ *Monitor*—Provides vital information about a NetWare server. Once loaded, this utility displays the information for server utilization, system resources, modules loaded, and a host of other valuable information to aid in troubleshooting your server.

◆ *Modules*—Displays a list of all modules currently running on the server. The modules command also displays the version and date for device driver modules, enabling you to determine if the current version of the driver is loaded on your server.

◆ *List Devices*—Verifies storage devices (tape backup unit and CD-ROM) that are recognized by NetWare.

◆ *Rconsole*—Allows remote connection to the server specified (if properly configured). Once connected, you can execute console commands as if you were at the server.

◆ *Nwconfig*—Changes the server's configuration and manages server operations.

◆ *Inetcfg*—Allows you to configure network boards and view configuration information.

◆ *Display Processors*—Lists all processors in the server and their status.

◆ *Ipxping*—Verifies connection to an **Internetwork Packet Exchange (IPX)** server on the network.

◆ *Ping*—Verifies connectivity between a server and device configured with an IP address.

◆ *Cpucheck*—Verifies the processor's speed, stepping, cache, and revision level.

◆ *Server –NS –NA*—Boots the server without loading the startup.ncf and autoexec.ncf files. At a console prompt, modules can be individually loaded to determine which module is causing the problem.

OBJECTIVES ON THE JOB

Hardware issues occur for various reasons. Knowing how to use common diagnostic tools ensures that your problem is quickly isolated and resolved. NetWare has a host of utilities to solve a variety of problems that can occur in your NetWare environment.

PRACTICE TEST QUESTIONS

1. **Which command allows you to configure network cards on the server?**
   a. inetcfg
   b. ipconfig
   c. ifconfig
   d. netconf

2. **Gary needs to find out which modules are running on the server. Which command can provide Gary with the information required? (Choose all that apply.)**
   a. rconsole
   b. modules
   c. monitor
   d. list devices

3. **Which command can be used to verify connection to an IPX server on the network?**
   a. ping
   b. ipxping
   c. track
   d. inetcfg

4. **Which of the following commands can be used to verify which storage devices are seen by NetWare?**
   a. ipxconfig
   b. ping
   c. traceroute
   d. list devices

5. **Which utility can be used to determine bottlenecks on your NetWare server?**
   a. Monitor
   b. Nwconfig
   c. Rconsole
   d. none of the above

6. **When running Server–ns –na at boot, which files will *not* be loaded? (Choose all that apply.)**
   a. startup.ncf
   b. netcfg.dll
   c. autoexec.ncf
   d. trace.ncf

7. **Jack needs to connect to a server downstairs to verify which modules are running on the server. Which of the following commands should Jack use?**
   a. ping
   b. RCONSOLE
   c. track
   d. traceroute

OBJECTIVES

6.2 Use diagnostic hardware and software tools and utilities (continued)

IDENTIFY COMMON DIAGNOSTIC TOOLS ACROSS THE FOLLOWING OPERATING SYSTEMS: UNIX, LINUX

UNDERSTANDING THE OBJECTIVE

With the increasing popularity of UNIX and Linux, you eventually will have to use software tools and utilities to troubleshoot a server running one of these OSs. Knowing how to access information about the server assists you in resolving the problem.

WHAT YOU REALLY NEED TO KNOW

◆ Many of the commands used to verify information in UNIX are also the same commands used by Linux. Commands vary depending on the version of UNIX or Linux you are running. Always check your documentation for commands and their usage. You should be familiar with the following commands and their uses in a UNIX or Linux environment:

◆ *ifconfig*—Displays the status of all configured interfaces on the server. This command can be used to enable or disable a network device.

◆ *ps*—Gives you information about current processes running on the server. You can verify the number of system resources being used by these processes.

◆ *sar*—Displays a report on system activity. Running this command with specific switches enables you to view reports for CPU, memory usage, and devices in your server.

◆ *df*—Shows the amount of used and available disk space on your server.

◆ *du*—Enables you to verify how much disk space files and directories use.

◆ *ping*—Verifies connectivity on networks running TCP/IP.

◆ *traceroute*—Records the route to a specified location and displays the amount of hops it takes to get to that location.

◆ *kill*—Terminates a process that is running on the server.

◆ *free*—This Linux-only command displays information about memory installed in the server.

◆ *top*—Provides you with information about processes running on the server and the memory allocated to those processes. This Linux-only command is run at the shell prompt.

OBJECTIVES ON THE JOB

UNIX and Linux are now common platforms in a networked environment. You must obtain as much information as possible on the platforms you are running. Doing so ensures that you have the necessary information required to diagnose and correct problems when they occur.

PRACTICE TEST QUESTIONS

1. **Which command displays the amount of used space and the amount of available space on your server's hard drives?**
   a. free
   b. df
   c. ifconfig
   d. top

2. **Which command can be used to configure network cards on a UNIX or Linux server?**
   a. free
   b. ipconfig
   c. ifconfig
   d. linuxmsd

3. **Jerry needs to determine what processes are running on his UNIX server. Which command will provide Jerry with the correct information?**
   a. ifconfig
   b. ps
   c. kill
   d. none of the above

4. **Which of the following commands displays a report for system activity?**
   a. ifconfig
   b. df
   c. kill
   d. sar

5. **The _____ command terminates a process running on a UNIX or Linux server.**
   a. free
   b. kill
   c. df
   d. du

6. **Which of the following commands are useful when troubleshooting a UNIX or Linux server? (Choose all that apply.)**
   a. traceroute
   b. kill
   c. ps
   d. df

7. **The _____ command displays processes running on a Linux server and the memory allocated to those processes.**
   a. du
   b. top
   c. free
   d. ds

6.2   Use diagnostic hardware and software tools and utilities (continued)

IDENTIFY COMMON DIAGNOSTIC TOOLS ACROSS THE FOLLOWING OPERATING SYSTEMS: IBM OS/2

UNDERSTANDING THE OBJECTIVE

As a server technician, you will be exposed to different server platforms. OS/2, although not as common as Windows 2000 or NetWare, can be found in many networked environments.

WHAT YOU REALLY NEED TO KNOW

◆ Be familiar with the following diagnostic utilities and their uses in an IBM OS/2 environment:

◆ *OS/2 Warpcenter*—Monitors CPU activity and available hard drive space on all partitions of the server.

◆ *Pstat*—Displays the status of processes, threads, and shared memory on the server and provides you with information on thread status, process ID, and system priority. This is a valuable tool when trying to determine which process is slowing the system.

◆ *Rmview*—Displays information about the hardware installed in your server and the system resources the hardware is using. This tool can be useful when trying to resolve hardware conflicts or when adding hardware to the server.

◆ *Syslevel*—Provides you with information about the revision level of the OS/2 software you are running.

◆ *Hard Disk Drive Monitor*—Monitors hard drives installed in the server. The monitor can detect potential failures on **self-monitoring, analysis, and reporting technology (SMART)** hard drives. Drives that have failed or have excessive errors have a flashing red light on the display indicating that there is a problem with the hard drive.

◆ *Chkdisk*—Detects and recovers lost clusters on the hard drives. This utility is used at the DOS prompt.

◆ *System Performance Monitor (SPM/2)*—Provides real-time information about processors, memory, swap activity, and many other server functions. This package can monitor both local and remote servers and provide you with detailed information when troubleshooting a problem. This collection of utilities is a separate software package developed by IBM.

OBJECTIVES ON THE JOB

Most networks consist of not one, but multiple network operating systems. It is not uncommon to find OS/2 servers within an organization's network structure. Technicians are constantly updating their knowledge base. Researching OS/2 provides you with the necessary tools to successfully troubleshoot and resolve related issues. Information about all the features, patches, and FAQs can be obtained from IBM's Web site.

PRACTICE TEST QUESTIONS

1. **Which of the following utilities monitors hard drive activity? (Choose all that apply.)**
    a. OS/2 Warpcenter
    b. Hard Disk Drive Monitor
    c. Chkdsk
    d. Pstat

2. **Which of the following commands displays the OS/2 software version installed on the server?**
    a. rmview
    b. sysibm
    c. winver
    d. syslevel

3. **Which command shows all processes running on the server and their status?**
    a. pstat
    b. rmview
    c. syslevel
    d. capture

4. **Which of the following can be used to recover lost clusters on an OS/2 server?**
    a. Rmview
    b. Rmstat
    c. Chkdsk
    d. Monitor

5. **Which utility can be used to display information about hardware installed in an OS/2 server?**
    a. Inetcfg
    b. Hwdcfg
    c. Rmview
    d. Tracehwd

6. **The Hard Disk Monitor can detect possible failures on _____ hard drives.**
    a. RAID
    b. SCSI
    c. IDE
    d. SMART

7. **Which of the following provides real-time information about OS/2 server functions?**
    a. Spm/2
    b. Pstat
    c. Rmview
    d. Console

6.2   Use diagnostic hardware and software tools and utilities (continued)

PERFORM SHUT DOWN ACROSS THE FOLLOWING OPERATING SYSTEMS: MICROSOFT WINDOWS NT/2000, NOVELL NETWARE, UNIX, LINUX, IBM OS/2

UNDERSTANDING THE OBJECTIVE

There are occasions when you have to shut down your server. Servers, like all computers, must be properly shut down to prevent damage to files and server hardware.

WHAT YOU REALLY NEED TO KNOW

◆ Never just power off a server. Doing so can corrupt files and eventually cause the server not to boot. Always use proper shutdown procedures for your OS.

◆ You should always inform users before shutting down your server. Users may be working with files or applications located on the server that must be closed before performing the shutdown.

◆ You must be able to perform shutdown procedures across the following OSs:

- Windows NT/2000

Select the Start button, and then select Shut Down.

Or

Press Ctrl+Alt+Del, and then select Shut Down.

- NetWare

NetWare 4.11

At the console prompt, type Down. At the console prompt, type Exit.

NetWare 5

At the console prompt, type Down.

- UNIX/Linux

Type shutdown –h now.

- IBM OS/2

At the OS/2 command window, type Shutdown. You also can right-click in the Workplace shell, select Shutdown, and then choose OK.

OBJECTIVES ON THE JOB

Shutting down a server is a common task that you must perform. Unless an emergency deems it necessary to do otherwise, you should always follow proper shutdown procedures when shutting down your server. Following proper shutdown procedures is essential to prevent data loss and file corruption. By informing your users of a server shutdown, you give them time to save their work and avoid having to reenter lost data.

PRACTICE TEST QUESTIONS

1. **Timothy needs to bring down the NetWare 5 database server for routine maintenance. What should Timothy do?**
   - a. Access a console prompt and type Down.
   - b. Notify users that the server will be shut down for maintenance.
   - c. Power the server off.
   - d. Access a console prompt and type Shutdown.

2. **What is the proper method for shutting down a NetWare 5 server?**
   - a. Press Ctrl+Alt+Del and select Shut Down.
   - b. Type shutdown – h now.
   - c. Access a console prompt and type Down.
   - d. none of the above

3. **What is the proper shutdown procedure for a UNIX or Linux server?**
   - a. trap –c -d
   - b. shutdown –h now
   - c. freeze –g0 -f
   - d. remove server

4. **The suspend \all command shuts down which of the following servers?**
   - a. Windows NT
   - b. Linux
   - c. NetWare
   - d. none of the above

5. **Which of the following methods can be used to properly shut down a Windows NT or Windows 2000 server? (Choose all that apply.)**
   - a. Select the Start button, and then select Shut Down.
   - b. From a DOS prompt, type Shutdown All.
   - c. Press Ctrl+Alt+Enter.
   - d. Press Ctrl+Alt+Del, and then select Shut Down.

6. **To properly shut down an OS/2 server, you should do which of the following?**
   - a. Type Down at the console prompt.
   - b. Press Ctrl+Alt three times.
   - c. Type Shutdown at the OS/2 command window.
   - d. none of the above

7. **Failure to properly shut down a server can cause which of the following problems?**
   - a. corrupt system files
   - b. corrupt data
   - c. data loss
   - d. all of the above

6.2 Use diagnostic hardware and software tools and utilities (continued)

REPLACE DEFECTIVE HARDWARE COMPONENTS AS APPROPRIATE

UNDERSTANDING THE OBJECTIVE

Defective components can cause system errors, data loss, and a host of other problems that can wreak havoc on your server. As a server technician, you must establish a method for identifying defective hardware and replacing it as appropriate.

WHAT YOU REALLY NEED TO KNOW

◆ First, you must establish that the hardware is truly defective. You should verify that all cables and power to the device are connected. A loose power connector could be the cause of the device failure. Cables also should be checked for bent or broken pins. Bad cables are notorious for causing intermittent device failures.

◆ Always thoroughly inspect the suspected hardware. Inspection can lead to the detection of broken components, burn marks, scratches, and other problems that could cause the device to malfunction. The smell of smoke is normally an indication that a component has burned out.

◆ Hardware diagnostics are an excellent way to determine if a hardware device is defective. The server or hardware vendor normally provides diagnostics for your hardware. Diagnostic software packages come on a variety of media. Downloads, CD-ROMs, and bootable floppies are the most common. Some server vendors load diagnostic software on a special partition, sometimes referred to as the utility partition, on the hard drive. Normally, the server has to be booted to the software to perform the diagnostics.

◆ Diagnostics can take a considerable amount of time to complete, depending on the level of diagnostics run on the server. Always factor in the time needed to complete the diagnostic before running one on a server.

◆ After a defective component has been removed from the server, you should place the item in a protective bag and mark it as bad. This prevents someone from using the defective component for a repair.

◆ Depending on your service level agreement or warranty, your server vendor may provide replacement parts for defective hardware. The server vendor almost always wants the defective component returned to the company. You should never throw away defective hardware.

OBJECTIVES ON THE JOB

When an organization's server goes down due to hardware failure, the organization's productivity level goes down as well. Remember that every minute a server is down costs the organization time and money. When called onsite to troubleshoot a server hardware issue, you must be able to determine what is causing the problem and bring the server back online as quickly as possible.

PRACTICE TEST QUESTIONS

1. **What should you do after you remove a defective part from the server?**
   a. Throw the part in the trash.
   b. Place the part in the cabinet with the other parts.
   c. Place the part on the workbench.
   d. Place the part in a protective bag and mark the part as bad.

2. **Scott has been called onsite to check a problem with a SCSI backplane. What is the first thing Scott should do after arriving onsite?**
   a. Remove the backplane and replace it with a new one.
   b. Verify that all cables and power connections are properly seated.
   c. Flash the backplane firmware.
   d. Run system diagnostics.

3. **A thorough inspection can lead to detection of which of the following problems? (Choose all that apply.)**
   a. burn marks
   b. broken components
   c. scratches
   d. peeling

4. **Which of the following can be used to detect defective hardware? (Choose all that apply.)**
   a. thorough inspection
   b. a screwdriver
   c. pliers
   d. diagnostic software

5. **Server diagnostic software can be on which of the following media? (Choose all that apply.)**
   a. floppies
   b. CD-ROMs
   c. memory
   d. utility partitions

6. **Your server vendor may replace a defective part under which of the following conditions? (Choose all that apply.)**
   a. service level agreement
   b. underperformance
   c. server warranty
   d. physical size mismatch

7. **Which of the following can cause a device to fail?**
   a. loose power connection
   b. bent or broken pins
   c. loose cables
   d. all of the above

6.2 Use diagnostic hardware and software tools and utilities (continued)

IDENTIFY DEFECTIVE FRUs AND REPLACE WITH CORRECT PART

UNDERSTANDING THE OBJECTIVE

Hard drives, network cards, memory, and many other components inside a server are considered **field replaceable units (FRUs)**. These items can be easily replaced onsite by a technician. When troubleshooting FRUs, you must ensure that the defective part is identified and replaced with the correct part.

WHAT YOU REALLY NEED TO KNOW

◆ You should ensure that components (adapters, hard drives, memory, cables, and so on) are properly seated. A device that is not properly seated can cause lockups, system errors, or an inability to boot the system.

◆ If an adapter or memory is causing the problem, try moving the item to a different slot. Doing so verifies that the problem lies with the component and not with the slot on the motherboard. If possible, try moving the device to another system to see if the problem follows the device.

◆ When handling components, always ensure that you are properly grounded. ESD can cause serious damage to the devices that you are trying to repair.

◆ Always verify that the correct software and driver for the hardware have been loaded. Did the device stop functioning after a patch or driver upgrade? Is the hardware passing diagnostics? Is the operating system giving an error specific to the device in question? The answers to these questions may indicate that it is not a hardware problem but a driver problem instead. Before deciding that the hardware is defective, try loading the latest driver for the hardware. The drivers can be obtained at the hardware vendor's Web site.

◆ After you have determined that a component is defective, you must ensure that the component is replaced with the correct part. The replacement part should be identical to the defective part. Manufacturers produce different types of hard drives, and a server may only take a specific type of memory. If the identical part is no longer available for your server, you should check with the hardware vendor to verify which component is an acceptable replacement. Sending the wrong part frustrates your customer and contributes to increased downtime for the server.

◆ Most organizations stock extra FRUs (memory, hard drives, network cards, and so on) in case an item is defective. This decreases the amount of server downtime for repair.

OBJECTIVES ON THE JOB

Replacing FRUs is a daily routine for some server technicians. Through proper diagnosis and verification, you can ensure that a defective component is identified and replaced with the correct component.

PRACTICE TEST QUESTIONS

1. **Which of the following items are considered FRUs? (Choose all that apply.)**
    a. hard drives
    b. network cards
    c. server chassis
    d. memory

2. **Mark is working on an issue involving a defective network card. The customer informs Mark that the problem started after he applied a patch to the server. What is causing the network card to fail?**
    a. RAM
    b. driver
    c. firmware
    d. none of the above

3. **What should you do when replacing a defective FRU? (Choose all that apply.)**
    a. Throw away the bad part.
    b. Replace the part with an identical part.
    c. Leave the part on the workbench.
    d. Ensure that you have the correct part number.

4. **Which of the following will stocking extra FRUs provide? (Choose all that apply.)**
    a. firmware RAM
    b. quick replacement for a defective part
    c. decreased server downtime
    d. increased hardware performance

5. **_____ can damage a FRU.**
    a. Diagnostics
    b. ESD
    c. Firmware
    d. CMOS changes

6. **Which of the following decreases server downtime?**
    a. never shutting down the server
    b. flashing the BIOS
    c. stocking extra FRUs
    d. swapping memory

7. **An adapter that is not properly seated can cause which of the following problems?**
    a. system errors
    b. server lockups
    c. boot problems
    d. all of the above

6.2 Use diagnostic hardware and software tools and utilities (continued)

INTERPRET ERROR LOGS, OPERATING SYSTEM ERRORS, HEALTH LOGS, AND CRITICAL EVENTS

UNDERSTANDING THE OBJECTIVE

Many problems that occur on a server can be tracked and diagnosed by obtaining information from logs and system errors for a specific device. You must be able to interpret information from logs and system errors to successfully troubleshoot an issue.

WHAT YOU REALLY NEED TO KNOW

◆ Be familiar with the following logs and errors:

◆ *Error logs*—Provide you with information for a specific device (tape backup unit, modem, and so on) that has encountered a problem during operation. Some devices generate an error log by default when an error occurs. Some devices require that you set error logging through the software provided for the device. You should check your device's documentation for information on how to set up and access your error logs.

◆ *OS errors*—Provide users with error messages when the operating system is functioning improperly. Network OSs, like Windows 2000 and NetWare, provide these error messages, which can range from simple to complex messages and can take some time to diagnose and resolve. OS vendors usually publish information regarding system errors and solutions on their Web sites.

◆ *Health logs*—Provide vital information about your server's hardware. Array status, processor temperature, and other important data can be logged for verification. All devices that are monitored have an agent that constantly polls the device at a predetermined interval. The agents are normally installed as part of a system management software package.

◆ *Critical errors*—Indicate there is a major problem with your server hardware. Failed hard drives in an array, an overheating processor, and exceeding server temperatures are all considered critical events. System monitoring software can be configured to send alerts to technicians and gracefully shut down the server, preventing further damage to server components.

OBJECTIVES ON THE JOB

The ability to interpret logs and error messages takes you a long way as a server technician and provides you with the information necessary to track and resolve issues that occur on your server. You should become familiar with all error codes and messages for all hardware and software in your server environment. Consider visiting your vendor's Web site for information on error messages and logs.

PRACTICE TEST QUESTIONS

1. **Todd received an error while working with Windows NT Server. The error message displayed a 0x7 error. Where can Todd find additional information on this error?**
   a. the hardware vendor's Web site
   b. the software vendor's Web site
   c. the server vendor's Web site
   d. none of the above

2. **For which of the following devices can you generate error logs? (Choose all that apply.)**
   a. modem
   b. network card
   c. hard drive
   d. device driver

3. **Receiving a(n) _____ error is normally a sign that there is a significant problem with your server.**
   a. application
   b. system
   c. critical
   d. security

4. **Which of the following tools can be used to troubleshoot an OS error? (Choose all that apply.)**
   a. server documentation
   b. OS vendor knowledge base
   c. multimeter
   d. none of the above

5. **When a critical error occurs, what can system monitoring do? (Choose all that apply.)**
   a. shut down a server
   b. send alerts to technicians
   c. clear the Registry
   d. remove corrupted data

6. **Which of the following items can be monitored with health logs? (Choose all that apply.)**
   a. server temperature
   b. fan speed
   c. chassis door
   d. drive arrays

6.2 Use diagnostic hardware and software tools and utilities (continued)

USE DOCUMENTATION FROM PREVIOUS TECHNICIAN SUCCESSFULLY

UNDERSTANDING THE OBJECTIVE

A good technician always documents an issue when troubleshooting. Documentation from previous technicians can be a valuable tool when working on an open issue.

WHAT YOU REALLY NEED TO KNOW

◆ When working with documentation to resolve an issue, you should verify that you are talking to the person who previously worked on the problem. If you discover that you are working with a different person, ensure that the person is aware of the issue's status.

◆ You should always read the previous technician's documentation thoroughly before attempting to troubleshoot an issue. Having the customer repeat steps that a technician previously covered is very frustrating. It also gives the customer an impression that the technician has no idea what has been done to address a specific issue.

◆ Always verify that the customer has completed the steps suggested by the previous technician. Verifying this information gives you the situation's status and aids you in determining your next step toward the issue's resolution.

◆ If you are unable to understand any of the documentation provided by the previous technician, you should contact the technician directly to clarify questionable information.

◆ Every step of your troubleshooting process should be documented. A process that may be considered irrelevant to one technician may assist another technician in resolving a problem.

◆ Always ensure that your log entries are professional. Most organizations retain log entries for their records. Most software packages used to record log entries do not let you change the entry after it has been entered into the system. Entries should always have the date, time, and name of the technician who logged the call. It is very easy for a manager or supervisor to discover who is making unprofessional entries in the logs.

◆ Organizations use different software packages to document issues. Be familiar with your organization's software and how to retrieve the documentation using the software in which it was created.

OBJECTIVES ON THE JOB

Log entries are the first documents that analysts and managers view before contacting a customer about an issue. Viewing all documentation for an incident gives you a better feel for the incident and provides you with vital information to help you resolve your customer's issue.

PRACTICE TEST QUESTIONS

1. **What should you do before troubleshooting an issue? (Choose all that apply.)**
   a. Verify the customer's information.
   b. Have the customer reboot the server.
   c. Flash the BIOS.
   d. Review all logs from previous technicians.

2. **If you are unable to understand a previous technician's log entries, you should:**
   a. Verify the information with the technician.
   b. Try to troubleshoot the problem anyway.
   c. Rewrite them to something more descriptive.
   d. Call the system administrator.

3. **When documenting an issue, your log entries should be _____. (Choose all that apply.)**
   a. detailed
   b. long
   c. professional
   d. stream of consciousness

4. **What information should be documented for an issue? (Choose all that apply.)**
   a. point of contact
   b. date
   c. technician's opinion
   d. technician who logged issue

5. **Joseph has just resolved an issue with a RAID controller. After completing the call, Joseph's supervisor asked him how he resolved the problem. Joseph cannot remember all the troubleshooting steps he performed. How could Joseph have prevented this problem?**
   a. Joseph should have taken a systems management class.
   b. Nothing, this problem could not have been prevented.
   c. Joseph should have documented the entire troubleshooting process.
   d. Joseph should have documented the procedures that he thought he would forget.

6. **Which of the following should use documentation when troubleshooting an issue? (Choose all that apply.)**
   a. technicians
   b. managers
   c. supervisors
   d. none of the above

7. **Using documentation from a previous technician can prevent which of the following?**
   a. frustrated customers
   b. repetition of troubleshooting procedures
   c. wasted time
   d. all of the above

6.2 Use diagnostic hardware and software tools and utilities (continued)

LOCATE AND EFFECTIVELY USE HOT TIPS

UNDERSTANDING THE OBJECTIVE

Today's technician has a wealth of resources and information available to assist him or her with any problem that may occur. You must know how to obtain and apply that information to resolve issues you may encounter.

WHAT YOU REALLY NEED TO KNOW

◆ Be familiar with the following resources and their usage:

◆ *Hot tips and fixes*—Assist you in resolving errors with hardware or software. These fixes range from making a simple configuration change to modifying operating system files like the Registry in Windows NT. Always verify that you have the correct fix for your problem before starting the process. You also should ensure that you have a complete backup of the server in case you encounter problems.

◆ *OS updates*—Help to resolve a variety of problems. Software vendors also release patches to enhance the functionality of the operating system. Patches are normally distributed by means of a CD-ROM or downloaded from the vendor's Web site. Always verify that a patch is compatible with your server platform. Never perform a patch before performing a complete backup of the server.

◆ *E-support*—Provides diagnosis and resolution to a problem. Not so long ago, getting a driver for a system meant waiting for the mail to arrive. With e-support, instructions, drivers, and utilities are sent via e-mail; they arrive in seconds, not days, no matter where the package is sent.

◆ *Internet*—Provides you with an excellent source of information. Vendors have constructed Web sites to assist with their customers' needs. These sites are filled with FAQs, updates, drivers, and many other tools to assist a technician when problems occur. You should have the manufacturer's Web address for every product (hardware and software) you support.

OBJECTIVES ON THE JOB

You will use many of the tools mentioned to accomplish your daily tasks. Hot fixes, e-support, and the Internet are three tools you must master. If you have encountered a problem with hardware or software, chances are that someone else has encountered the same problem and published the solution to the problem on the Web. After determining what equipment you have in your server environment, consider visiting your vendors' Web sites for information or utilities that can enhance the performance of your server.

PRACTICE TEST QUESTIONS

1. **Vickie has been given the task of patching the server. What should Vickie do before performing the patch?**
   a. Reboot the server.
   b. Perform a complete backup of the server.
   c. Flash the BIOS.
   d. Do nothing.

2. **Sending a file via e-support normally takes _____ to deliver.**
   a. hours
   b. weeks
   c. seconds
   d. months

3. **Which of the following can normally and easily be found at a vendor's Web site? (Choose all that apply.)**
   a. patches
   b. FAQs
   c. phone numbers of employees
   d. drivers

4. **Patches are normally distributed through which of the following media? (Choose all that apply.)**
   a. CD-ROMs
   b. downloads
   c. floppies
   d. none of the above

5. **Hot tips are usually which of the following items?**
   a. an executable file
   b. a batch file
   c. a documented process
   d. someone's opinion

6. **The Internet can provide an excellent source of detailed information about which of the following items? (Choose all that apply.)**
   a. troubleshooting tools
   b. system utilities
   c. driver updates
   d. known product issues

6.2 Use diagnostic hardware and software tools and utilities (continued)

GATHER RESOURCES TO GET PROBLEM SOLVED • IDENTIFY SITUATIONS REQUIRING CALL FOR ASSISTANCE • ACQUIRE APPROPRIATE DOCUMENTATION

UNDERSTANDING THE OBJECTIVE

A server technician uses many resources to resolve a problem. Troubleshooting an issue is a small part of a larger process. You must follow a predetermined process when trying to resolve an issue and ask yourself specific questions that gather the information that you need.

WHAT YOU REALLY NEED TO KNOW

◆ *Do I have the necessary resources to resolve the problem?* Without the necessary resources, you have a very slim chance of resolving the problem. You must ensure that you have all drivers, files, utilities, and any other items required to successfully resolve the problem. You should identify everyone involved in the process of resolving the issue. Customers, vendors, and technicians who have experience working with similar issues can provide you with valuable information.

◆ *Do I have the appropriate documentation for the issue?* Before troubleshooting an issue, you must acquire all documentation necessary to resolve the problem. If working on an open issue, you should review all previous log entries on the issue. Check with all technicians involved to ensure that the information contained in the log entries is correct. Documentation from the hardware vendor gives you detailed information on configurations and settings for a specific piece of server hardware.

◆ *What do I do when things go wrong?* When working on an issue, you may encounter a problem that you are unable to resolve. You must know when to escalate an issue to the appropriate person. Escalating the issue may mean calling your supervisors to inform them of the problem or contacting the hardware vendor. Most organizations have a process flow chart that gives detailed instructions for properly escalating an issue. Regardless, you should always use sound judgment when determining whether to escalate an issue.

OBJECTIVES ON THE JOB

Before troubleshooting begins, you must establish a foundation. Ensure that you have the available resources and documentation to build a foundation for troubleshooting an issue. Eventually, all technicians encounter a problem that they are unable to resolve. Spending time trying to resolve an issue that is beyond your level of knowledge not only wastes time but costs your customer money as well. Remember that in most cases, all work ceases until the server is repaired. Escalating the issue ensures that the server is returned to normal operation as quickly as possible.

PRACTICE TEST QUESTIONS

1. **Which of the following are considered resources for resolving an issue? (Choose all that apply.)**
   a. drivers
   b. the vendor's Web site
   c. other technicians
   d. customers

2. **John has been assigned an issue that has been open for three days. Four technicians worked on the issue prior to John. What should John do to help resolve the issue? (Choose all that apply.)**
   a. Read all previous log entries.
   b. Start working on the issue right away.
   c. Gather information from the previous technicians involved.
   d. Gather the necessary documentation to resolve the problem.

3. **Sam has been given the task of repairing a server. When Sam arrives onsite, he discovers that the server is in a cluster configuration. Sam has never worked with clustering. What should Sam do?**
   a. Try to resolve the issue anyway.
   b. Power down both servers.
   c. Inform his supervisor of the issue.
   d. Run diagnostics on the problem server.

4. **Which of the following can be used to escalate an issue?**
   a. hardware vendor
   b. supervisor
   c. process flow chart
   d. all of the above

5. **Eric has been working on an open issue with a customer. When Eric called the customer back, a different person answered the phone. The person informs Eric that he is now working on the issue. What should Eric do? (Choose all that apply.)**
   a. Gather information from his new contact.
   b. Start troubleshooting the issue.
   c. Verify that previous troubleshooting steps were completed.
   d. Ask to speak to the previous point of contact.

6. **Jess has been given the task of configuring an array for a customer. After running the utility, he discovers that he has never seen this utility before. What should Jess do? (Choose all that apply.)**
   a. Try to configure the array.
   b. Call the RAID controller vendor.
   c. Inform his supervisor of the issue.
   d. Leave the customer's site.

6.2 Use diagnostic hardware and software tools and utilities (continued)

DESCRIBE HOW TO PERFORM REMOTE TROUBLESHOOTING FOR A WAKE-ON-LAN

UNDERSTANDING THE OBJECTIVE

Most organizations have multiple locations that are networked together in some fashion. Maintaining multiple locations can be quite a task for a technician. A wake-on-LAN simplifies the task of managing systems at remote locations.

WHAT YOU REALLY NEED TO KNOW

◆ A **wake-on-LAN** is a feature of the **Wired for Management (WfM)** system created by Intel and IBM. Wake-on-LAN-compatible software enables a technician to power up a remote system and perform various activities (maintenance, virus checking, configuration changes, and so on) to the system. When all tasks are completed, the technician can remotely power down the system.

◆ All of the following items must be compatible with the WfM specification in order to use the features of a wake-on-LAN:
  - Motherboard and BIOS
  - Operating system
  - Power supply
  - Network adapter

◆ The wake-on-LAN adapter has a special cable that attaches from the adapter to a special socket on the motherboard that supports wake-on-LANs. Some LAN-on-motherboard NICs support wake-on-LANs. Your hardware vendor has additional information about your hardware and what features are supported.

◆ Special WfM software packages are used to perform all tasks associated with wake-on-LANs. When used with other interfaces like **Desktop Management Interface (DMI)**, you are able to view important information about the system you are accessing. This information can simplify the task of inventory and system monitoring. Be familiar with the different types of software packages that use wake-on-LAN technology.

OBJECTIVES ON THE JOB

A network using wake-on-LAN technology assists you in managing your day-to-day activities. You are provided instant access to client systems on the network, regardless of whether the client is local or remote. Wake-on-LAN features reduce the amount of time required to manage a remote location by centralizing many activities. IBM and Intel Web sites contain valuable information about wake-on-LAN. Consider the advantages of implementing wake-on-LAN technology in your server environment.

PRACTICE TEST QUESTIONS

1. **WfM is an acronym for which of the following?**
   a. Windows for Masses
   b. Wired for Management
   c. Web Formatted Media
   d. Windows Format Media

2. **Which of the following items must be compatible to implement a wake-on-LAN? (Choose all that apply.)**
   a. motherboard
   b. power supply
   c. server chassis
   d. BIOS

3. **A wake-on-LAN adapter has a special cable that attaches from the adapter to the _____.**
   a. power supply
   b. motherboard
   c. SCSI backplane
   d. modem

4. **DMI is an acronym for which of the following?**
   a. Default Mask Interrupt
   b. Domain Management Interface
   c. Desktop Management Interface
   d. Desktop Manual Interface

5. **WfM technology was developed through a joint venture between which two companies?**
   a. Dell and IBM
   b. Compaq and Dell
   c. IBM and Intel
   d. IBM and Compaq

6. **Which of the following tasks can be performed remotely using WfM technology? (Choose all that apply.)**
   a. backups
   b. system updates
   c. virus scans
   d. system shutdowns

7. **Which of the following can provide you with the information about wake-on-LAN? (Choose all that apply.)**
   a. OS vendor's Web site
   b. server vendor's Web site
   c. NIC vendor's Web site
   d. server documentation

OBJECTIVES

6.2   Use diagnostic hardware and software tools and utilities (continued)

DESCRIBE HOW TO PERFORM REMOTE TROUBLESHOOTING FOR A REMOTE ALERT

UNDERSTANDING THE OBJECTIVE

When you receive a remote alert, you must be able to troubleshoot and resolve the problem. Many issues that occur on a remote server can be resolved without having to visit the server's location.

WHAT YOU REALLY NEED TO KNOW

- ◆ **Remote alerts** can be configured to provide you with vital information about your server's status. Hard drive capacity, system errors, and server temperature are just a few of the alerts that can be configured. Configure alerts by setting a specific threshold for an object. After that threshold is met or exceeded, an alert is generated. When configuring an alert, you must also specify who will receive the alert message when an error occurs.
- ◆ An alert message normally consists of the following items:
  - Originator—The server that has experienced the problem
  - Recipient—The person(s) who received the message
  - Date/time—The date and time the error occurred
  - Description—A brief description of the actual error
- ◆ The details from an alert message provide you with information to begin your troubleshooting procedures.
- ◆ After you receive an alert, you can connect to the server that has encountered an error. After a connection has been established, you are able to retrieve additional information about the problem. An alert message gives only a very brief description of a problem that may require additional information to resolve. System logs can provide you with a wealth of information that helps you identify and isolate the problem.
- ◆ There are a host of remote management tools that can be used to resolve a problem. The OS has native tools and add-on packages that can be purchased for additional flexibility.
- ◆ Some organizations use third-party software for remote management. Be familiar with your organization's software and its capabilities.

OBJECTIVES ON THE JOB

The number of servers that a technician is responsible for can be quite a task to manage. By using alerts and remote management tools, you will be able to connect to and resolve problems on a server no matter where the server resides, reducing the time it takes to resolve an issue.

PRACTICE TEST QUESTIONS

1. **Which of the following items can be configured to alert a technician if a problem occurs? (Choose all that apply.)**
   a. hard drive capacity
   b. server temperature
   c. system errors
   d. device failure

2. **Which of the following are alert message components? (Choose all that apply.)**
   a. originator
   b. date
   c. time
   d. backup server

3. **Alerts are configured when setting _____ on objects.**
   a. jumpers
   b. switches
   c. thresholds
   d. scripts

4. **An alert message consists of which of the following components? (Choose all that apply.)**
   a. orginator
   b. server SID
   c. date/time
   d. 128-bit encryption

5. **Errors can be resolved by using which of the following remote management tools? (Choose all that apply.)**
   a. native operating system tools
   b. add-on packages
   c. third-party software
   d. error checking cards

6. **A remote alert gives you a(n) _____ description of a problem.**
   a. detailed
   b. encrypted
   c. brief
   d. encoded

6.3   Identify bottlenecks

IDENTIFY BOTTLENECKS

UNDERSTANDING THE OBJECTIVE

Performance is always a vital aspect of your server and network environments. Your servers and networks should perform at an optimal level at all times. Bottlenecks can cause problems with the performance of your network. As a server technician, you must be able to identify and resolve conflicts caused by bottlenecks.

WHAT YOU REALLY NEED TO KNOW

- ◆ Memory, processors, disk arrays, and adapters all play a critical role in server performance. Processor cache, incorrect RAID array type, and insufficient memory can bring the server to a crawl and cause access and performance problems.

- ◆ You must ensure that the hardware installed in your server does not decrease your server's capability. For example, a 33 **megahertz (MHz)** card in a 66 MHz slot slows the bus to 33 MHz, causing a significant decrease in server performance. Researching information about specific hardware provides you with the necessary information about your server and its hardware.

- ◆ You should always ensure that your server and OS are configured correctly. All of your BIOS settings should be configured for the optimal performance of your server. OS configurations should be verified to ensure that settings (virtual memory, caching, and so on) allow the server to perform efficiently. You can obtain documentation from your software vendor that provides information about configuring your OS for maximum performance.

- ◆ Server baselines are valuable tools for ensuring that your server is performing at the desired level. A baseline should be performed when a server is implemented into the network. As your organization grows, you can perform additional baselines and compare the information received to the information obtained in the earlier baseline. This information can be used to highlight problems in server performance.

- ◆ There are many third-party performance monitoring tools on the market today, but most OSs have native performance monitoring tools that can assist you with identifying and resolving bottlenecks.

OBJECTIVES ON THE JOB

Your server must process and move data across the network efficiently. By identifying and removing bottlenecks, you help to ensure that your server and network perform as they were designed to perform. If users make statements like "I remember when the network used to run a lot faster than it does now," this could be an indication of bottlenecks within your network. Using the proper tools and documentation assists you in identifying the source of the problem and tuning your server and network to optimal performance.

PRACTICE TEST QUESTIONS

1. **Which of the following can cause bottlenecks in a server? (Choose all that apply.)**
   a. server chassis
   b. processor
   c. server fans
   d. hard drives

2. **John installed an NT server three months ago. Since then, 15 users have been added to the network. John wants to know if the server is performing as efficiently as when it was first installed on the network. John performed a baseline when the server was installed. How can John check server performance?**
   a. Reboot the server.
   b. Perform a server baseline and compare it to the previous baseline.
   c. Compare the baseline to baselines for other systems on the same network.
   d. Have a user access an application.

3. **Which of the following increases server performance? (Choose all that apply.)**
   a. configuring your BIOS settings correctly
   b. adding additional fans to the server
   c. properly configuring your OS
   d. adding the appropriate hardware to your server

4. **Performance problems can be caused by which of the following? (Choose all that apply.)**
   a. increased traffic
   b. insufficient RAM
   c. additional CPUs
   d. hard drives at 98% capacity

5. **Todd is running an SQL server that is accessed by 50 users. What Web site should Todd visit to obtain information about fine-tuning his SQL server?**
   a. the hardware vendor's Web site
   b. the software vendor's Web site
   c. Todd's company Web site
   d. none of the above

6. **Which tools can be used to identify and resolve bottlenecks? (Choose all that apply.)**
   a. third-party software
   b. hardware diagnostics
   c. OS utilities
   d. No such software currently exists.

7. **Which of the following can assist you with server performance?**
   a. third-party software
   b. the vendor's Web site
   c. native OS utilities
   d. all of the above

6.4   Identify and correct misconfigurations and/or upgrades

IDENTIFY AND CORRECT MISCONFIGURATIONS AND/OR UPGRADES

UNDERSTANDING THE OBJECTIVE

A server that has been configured or upgraded improperly can experience problems ranging from system errors to boot failure. When it is determined that a device has an incorrect configuration or upgrade, you must be able to take the necessary steps to correct the problem.

WHAT YOU REALLY NEED TO KNOW

◆ When your server POSTs, it provides you with valuable information about your server's setup. SCSI and RAID controllers also show device information that can be used to troubleshoot a configuration issue.

◆ Your server's System Setup Utility and/or EISA Configuration Utility can provide you with information about the hardware, IRQs, memory addresses, and other system settings. SCSI controllers also have a BIOS utility that provides you with information about the SCSI ID of a device residing on the SCSI bus. If you are unable to see a device using this utility, there is a possibility that the device has been configured with a SCSI ID that is already in use. Changing the SCSI ID for the device to an available ID and ensuring that the SCSI bus is terminated properly normally resolves this problem.

◆ Some misconfigurations can be easily changed. For example, an adapter that is residing on the wrong IRQ can be changed in the System Setup Utility and/or the EISA Configuration Utility. Some adapters function properly only on certain IRQs. Reviewing your adapter documentation assists you in configuring the adapter correctly.

◆ Correcting an upgrade may not be as easy as correcting a hardware configuration problem. Depending on the type of upgrade performed, correction can range from a simple file replacement to completely restoring the server. This is why it is important to perform a complete backup of the server before attempting to perform an upgrade. You also should verify the backup to ensure that it was successful.

◆ There are times when changing a misconfiguration means scheduling an appropriate time to change the configuration. For example, changing a RAID 0/1 to RAID 5 can be quite a task once the data has been loaded to the server and all users are accessing that data. When scheduling the update, you should give yourself ample time to complete the update and resolve any problems that may occur.

OBJECTIVES ON THE JOB

As a technician, you will encounter various configuration issues. By identifying the problem, establishing a corrective action, and scheduling an appropriate time to resolve the problem, you ensure that the issue is diagnosed and resolved efficiently. You should consider reviewing the hardware and software configuration on your servers to verify that all settings are configured for optimal performance.

PRACTICE TEST QUESTIONS

1. **A misconfiguration or upgrade can cause which of the following problems? (Choose all that apply.)**
   a. system errors
   b. boot problems
   c. data loss
   d. viruses

2. **Mashone has been given the task of performing a software upgrade on the Exchange server. What should Mashone do first?**
   a. Tell all users to log off the network.
   b. Reboot the server.
   c. Perform a complete backup of the server.
   d. Start the upgrade.

3. **Gary has to change the IRQ settings for a network card that was configured incorrectly. Which utility can Gary use to perform this task?**
   a. System diags
   b. System Setup
   c. SCSI BIOS
   d. Ntsetup.exe

4. **Which of the following can be used to correct a device that was configured improperly? (Choose all that apply.)**
   a. MS DOS
   b. SCSI BIOS
   c. NVRAM
   d. SSU

5. **Which of the following is important when verifying a SCSI device? (Choose all that apply.)**
   a. Each device should have a unique SCSI ID.
   b. The SCSI bus should be properly terminated.
   c. The SCSI device should be near the server fans.
   d. Run Scsiupdate.exe before verification.

6. **Ted received a call from a customer complaining about his hard drive space. The customer ordered four drives in a RAID 5 configuration. When the customer boots the server, the BIOS displays a message that two logical drives are found and two logical drives are handled by the BIOS. What is the customer's problem?**
   a. The EISA settings are incorrect.
   b. The RAID controller is bad.
   c. The RAID array is configured incorrectly.
   d. Nothing, the customer's configuration is correct.

7. **Which of the following statements are true about misconfigurations? (Choose all that apply.)**
   a. They are always easy to fix.
   b. They can be avoided by using proper documentation.
   c. They cannot affect server performance.
   d. They should be changed as soon as possible.

6.5   Determine if the problem is hardware, software or virus related

DETERMINE IF THE PROBLEM IS HARDWARE, SOFTWARE OR VIRUS RELATED

UNDERSTANDING THE OBJECTIVE

Almost all server problems, with a few exceptions, are due to problems with hardware, software, or a virus. A technician must be able to identify where the root of the problem lies and provide a corrective action.

WHAT YOU REALLY NEED TO KNOW

◆ Hardware problems can normally be identified when a device fails during normal operation or is not recognized at startup. Some hardware failures cause the OS to generate an error if the OS is trying to communicate with the device and the device fails to respond.

◆ Many hardware devices have **light-emitting diodes (LEDs)** that can be used to verify that a problem exists. Be familiar with the error codes and indicators for your hardware.

◆ Adapters are notorious for causing NO POST NO VIDEO problems. When uncertain which adapter is causing the problem, try removing all of the adapters and replacing them one at a time until the bad adapter is identified.

◆ Hardware diagnostics are excellent tools for identifying hardware problems. You should always maintain the latest diagnostic software for your server.

◆ Software problems can cause a server to perform slowly or crash if the problem is severe. Many problems can be resolved by researching the error message generated by the OS or application. Applications that are incompatible with each other cause errors when run at the same time on a server. Your software vendor's Web site can provide you with information for resolving software errors.

◆ Always thoroughly investigate a software error. Software errors can occur when a system has been infected with a virus.

◆ Viruses launch malicious attacks on servers and networks. Be familiar with the different types of viruses and their symptoms. A virus can cripple an organization and cost a considerable amount of time and money to resolve.

◆ Anti-virus software is an excellent tool for identifying and cleaning an infected server. You should run anti-virus software regularly to ensure that your system is clean. You should also update your software to ensure that you have an updated list of discovered viruses.

OBJECTIVES ON THE JOB

You must master the skills for identifying the root cause of a problem. Knowing why an error occurred assists you in determining what steps need to be taken and selecting the necessary tools to resolve the problem.

PRACTICE TEST QUESTIONS

1. **Which of the following can be caused by software problems? (Choose all that apply.)**
   a. slow system performance
   b. system errors
   c. overheating
   d. server crashes

2. **Scott believes that the NIC in his server has failed. What can Scott do to verify that the card is bad? (Choose all that apply.)**
   a. Move the card to a different slot.
   b. Run hardware diagnostics.
   c. Check the indicator lights on the card.
   d. Flash the network card BIOS.

3. **Patrick is having problems with his SQL server. When the server tries to access files from a Lotus database, the server locks and has to be rebooted. What type of error causes this type of problem?**
   a. hardware
   b. software
   c. virus
   d. network

4. **Which of the following statements are true about viruses? (Choose all that apply.)**
   a. They can spread across an entire network.
   b. They cannot be detected with software.
   c. They can cause system errors.
   d. They are not a threat to a server environment.

5. **Dianne is investigating a server boot problem. While trying to resolve the problem, Dianne receives calls from users in three different departments complaining of the same problem. What could possibly be the cause of this problem?**
   a. hardware
   b. software
   c. virus
   d. application issues

6. **While working within an application, Sara receives an insufficient memory error. What type of error is causing the problem?**
   a. software
   b. hardware
   c. virus
   d. networking

7. **Which of the following can cause software problems? (Choose all that apply.)**
   a. jumper settings
   b. viruses
   c. applications
   d. LEDs

7.1 Plan for disaster recovery

PLAN FOR REDUNDANCY

UNDERSTANDING THE OBJECTIVE

Redundancy is imperative to server management and is especially important in the high-availability class of servers. Because it is the most basic component of disaster recovery, without it there is no disaster recovery plan. This section highlights the methods of ensuring hardware redundancy in the event of any type of failure that can result in data loss or loss of networking capabilities.

WHAT YOU REALLY NEED TO KNOW

◆ Redundancy, in the server hardware sense, can be best defined as the provision of multiple, interchangeable components to perform a single function in order to cope with failures and errors.

◆ Server manufacturers provide redundancy options in systems by factory installing multiple power supplies, fan packs, and so on.

◆ It is important to note that data redundancy is crucial. By utilizing a hardware RAID controller and configuration, the risk of data loss is greatly minimized. To employ this option, multiple hard drives must be installed and configured. Review the various levels of RAID to determine the best solution for your data type and business needs.

◆ Hot swapping hard drives is also an option for multiple hard drives.

◆ It is important to note that when configuring multiple hard drives, the drives should be the same size and type. RAID controllers use the smallest drive's size as the size of all the drives. Therefore, if you use two 9 GB hard drives with one 2 GB hard drive, the two larger drives are only recognized as 2 GB each.

◆ System cooling is another very important factor to consider. System fans are usually redundant in the server from the manufacturer. If they are not offered as standard, they usually are offered as an optional item.

◆ Many server system boards have on-board network adapters. Utilizing additional adapters and configuring a fault-tolerant network solution are easy ways to implement redundancy for network adapters.

◆ Many server system boards also contain configurations of two or more processors. Redundant CPUs are utilized most in companies in which high availability is crucial.

OBJECTIVES ON THE JOB

Ensuring the stability of the server environment, the data contained within, and the access users have to that data is the server technician's responsibility. Many solutions are available to enable the technician to better ensure the functionality of the server as well as recovery in the event of a hardware failure. Redundant hardware solutions offer the ability to keep the server up and running while an alert is sent to the administrator indicating the need for repair. This minimizes the impact of any hardware failure on the business, its users, and the important data the server contains.

PRACTICE TEST QUESTIONS

1. **Rob has installed his server in a rack with a UPS attached and configured to take over in the event of power loss or failure. What is another option he should consider to ensure that the server maintains power under all circumstances?**
   a. multiple UPSs
   b. multiple NICs
   c. redundant power supplies
   d. redundant fans

2. **The new network administrator arrived onsite to perform a server upgrade. He noticed that the server had a RAID controller and multiple hard drives configured in a RAID 5 array. Which of the following statements is true?**
   a. The data on the server is not redundant.
   b. The data on the server is redundant due to the RAID 5 configuration.
   c. The drives in the array are mirrored.
   d. The drives in the array do not contain parity.

3. **Arthur noticed that the room for the new server rack installation was extremely warm. Which of the following options would help to keep the server climate under control?**
   a. redundant fans inside the servers
   b. redundant power supplies
   c. redundant hard drives
   d. all of the above

4. **A network server was installed and configured as a primary domain controller (PDC). As the server's main function is to provide user validation, which of the following statements is true regarding redundancy?**
   a. Only one NIC is needed to provide users with sufficient access and validation.
   b. The server should be configured into a Token Ring network to ensure constant access for users.
   c. The server should be configured with multiple NICs or a fault-tolerant network solution to provide continued validation for users in the event one NIC fails to function properly.
   d. A workstation should be connected and configured to provide validation if the server fails.

5. **Which of the following provides redundancy in the event of a hardware malfunction?**
   a. multiple processors
   b. multiple network adapters
   c. multiple power supplies
   d. all of the above

7.1   Plan for disaster recovery (continued)

USE THE TECHNIQUE OF HOT SWAP, WARM SWAP AND HOT SPARE TO ENSURE AVAILABILITY

UNDERSTANDING THE OBJECTIVE

Another form of redundancy, which is highly utilized in the server environment, is the action of providing additional hard drives and other components in the event that the main hard drive or component fails. These configurations have different names depending on the purpose of the component. This section highlights the use of hot fix, hot swap, warm swap, and hot spare configurations and the purpose of these techniques.

WHAT YOU REALLY NEED TO KNOW

- ◆ **Hot fixing** involves marking sectors in poor condition as bad and remapping the data to spare sectors during normal operation. Usually an OS (such as NetWare) rereads every block it writes to disk while it holds the data to be written in memory.

- ◆ In the case of an error, the data block is written to a spare area on the disk. Some SCSI drives can automatically move the data in sectors that are becoming hard to read to spare sectors without the user, OS, or even the SCSI host adapter being aware of it.

- ◆ Hot fixing became less utilized with the widespread use of hard disk drives with built-in error correction and bad block remapping.

- ◆ Hot swapping is the ability of a SCSI RAID controller's software suite to allow removal and replacement of a disk drive while users are online and accessing data (active I/O).

- ◆ All hot-swap, hot-spare disk drives are sold in 80-pin **SCA**-2 SCSI interface configurations. Hard drives and enclosures must be compatible with hot-swap level 4 compliance.

- ◆ Not all hard drive enclosures or drive bays support hot swap—especially with removable drive trays. You must confirm hot-swap capability with the component manufacturer before removing drives in an operational storage solution.

- ◆ A warm swap is a device that can be pulled from a system and exchanged while the system power is on and the unit is still operating. A warm swap can be a hard drive, a circuit board, a power supply, a processor, and so on.

- ◆ Hot spare is a RAID architecture feature that allows an extra hard drive to be included on a RAID controller in case of sudden drive failure.

- ◆ By definition, a spare device is not preconfigured as part of the RAID array. A spare drive is available to automatically reconstruct data in the event any single drive fails during normal system operation.

OBJECTIVES ON THE JOB

Performing the discussed techniques in a server environment further enhances the technician's ability to maintain a functional system and to reduce downtime in the event of hardware failures.

PRACTICE TEST QUESTIONS

1. **Which of the following techniques is used predominantly on a NetWare server?**
   a. hot spare
   b. warm swap
   c. hot swap
   d. hot fix

2. **The new network administrator arrived onsite to perform a server upgrade. He noticed that the server had a RAID controller and multiple hard drives configured in a RAID 5 array. What is a redundancy option he can use for an additional hard drive?**
   a. hot spare
   b. warm swap
   c. hot swap
   d. hot fix

3. **Which of the following components can be replaced in a hot-swap environment?**
   a. fans inside the servers
   b. power supplies
   c. hard drives
   d. all of the above

4. **Robert thought he needed to configure the OS to write bad sectors of data to a particular location on the hard drive. With new hard drives that have built-in error correcting, which of the following is true?**
   a. He doesn't need to do anything at all; the drives will do this automatically.
   b. He should perform the configuration for writing the bad data from within the BIOS of the hard drive controller.
   c. He needs to install an OS that allows him to use the error correcting feature on the drives.
   d. He should perform the configuration for writing the bad data from within the system BIOS.

5. **The hot spare is a feature of _____ architecture.**
   a. UPS
   b. NIC
   c. RAID
   d. all of the above

6. **One of the tasks involved in the setup of the newest server on the network was to configure the hot-swappable hard drives in the system. Of the following, which component should be validated for this configuration?**
   a. hard drives
   b. hard drive enclosures
   c. backplanes
   d. all of the above

7.1 Plan for disaster recovery (continued)

USE THE CONCEPTS OF FAULT TOLERANCE/FAULT RECOVERY TO CREATE A DISASTER RECOVERY PLAN

UNDERSTANDING THE OBJECTIVE

The need to make informed decisions about system requirements and determine what resources are available to meet those requirements is the first step in designing a fault-tolerant server environment. When planning for a highly available and fault-tolerant deployment, all points of failure and work should be considered to eliminate any single point of failure. Redundant power supplies, dual disk controllers, multiple network interface cards (multihoming), and fault-tolerant disk arrays (RAID) are all strategies that should be employed.

WHAT YOU REALLY NEED TO KNOW

◆ The biggest failure point for any network is its power supply. Including a UPS with the initial order of server equipment addresses this concern.

◆ Except for level 0, RAID is a mechanism for storing information on a group of hard disks such that even if one hard disk in the group fails, no information is lost. Some RAID arrangements go even further and provide protection in the event of multiple hard disk failures.

◆ Although a hardware RAID configuration increases overall fault tolerance, it still can leave a single point of failure—the disk controller itself—in your disk subsystem. Failures of the disk controller are less common, but they do occur. Many hardware RAID systems are based on a single multiple-channel controller.

◆ Hardware RAID systems can provide for both hot-swap and hot-spare capabilities. A hot-swap disk system allows failed hard disks to be removed and a replacement disk inserted into the array without powering down the system or rebooting the server.

◆ Network load balancing (called Windows Load Balancing Service in Microsoft Windows NT 4.0) allows TCP/IP-based applications to be spread dynamically across servers. If a particular server fails, the load and connections to that server are dynamically balanced to the remaining servers.

◆ Server clusters depend on a shared SCSI or Fibre Channel–attached disk array between the nodes of the cluster. Each server in the cluster is connected to the shared resource, and the common database that manages the clustering is stored on this shared resource.

OBJECTIVES ON THE JOB

Building a highly available and fault-tolerant system requires evaluation of requirements and resources to eliminate single points of failure within the system. Ensure that recovery procedures are clearly understood and practiced to reduce recovery time in the event of a failure. The server technician's role is to plan these tasks and ensure that the procedures are followed as planned.

PRACTICE TEST QUESTIONS

1. Susan is responsible for the installation of a new server. One of the concerns raised by a technician is occasional power sagging in the building. Which of the following would alleviate those problems?
   a. hot spare
   b. UPS
   c. RAID
   d. hot fix

2. Which RAID level is not fault tolerant?
   a. RAID 0
   b. RAID 1
   c. RAID 5
   d. RAID 10

3. Bob is learning how to configure a cluster environment. Which of the following would be a shared resource for the nodes?
   a. fans inside the servers
   b. power supplies
   c. hard drives
   d. SCSI or Fibre Channel

4. While Tom was configuring a RAID 5 array, he realized he could perform this on both channels of the RAID controller. Which point of failure has not been considered with this configuration?
   a. hard drive failure
   b. UPS failure
   c. RAID controller failure
   d. fan failure

5. The terms load balancing and multihoming apply to:
   a. UPS
   b. NIC
   c. RAID
   d. all of the above

6. Which of the following does not need to be considered when designing a fault-tolerant environment for a server?
   a. power supplies
   b. NICs
   c. network cable
   d. RAID

7.1 Plan for disaster recovery (continued)

USE THE CONCEPTS OF FAULT TOLERANCE/FAULT RECOVERY TO CREATE A DISASTER RECOVERY PLAN (CONTINUED)

UNDERSTANDING THE OBJECTIVE

The amount of hardware failures and potential data loss can be minimized by the use of fault-tolerant techniques, such as the prediction technology available from hard drive manufacturers today. This technology provides the technician with ample notification in the event that a hard drive failure is likely to occur. This provides the technician with ample time to obtain a suitable replacement hard drive, schedule enough downtime for the replacement process, and notify users of the event.

WHAT YOU REALLY NEED TO KNOW

- ◆ The main purpose of reliability prediction technology is to anticipate the failure of a disk drive with sufficient notice to allow a system, or user, to back up data prior to a hard drive failure.
- ◆ Generally, hard drives with reliability prediction technology report a condition as either good or failing.
- ◆ There are two different classifications of failures:
  1. Predictable failures are characterized by degradation of certain functions over time. Examples of these functions are spin-up time, reallocated sector count, and seek time performance.
  2. Nonpredictable failures, such as electronic and mechanical problems, occur quickly. A power surge resulting in chip or circuit failure is an example of a sudden problem that is not predictable.
- ◆ Improvements in design process, quality, and manufacturing are options for decreasing the incidence of nonpredictable failures.
- ◆ Mechanical failures, which are mainly predictable failures, account for 60% of drive failures.
- ◆ If 60% of failing hard drives are losing functionality and possibly critical data due to "predictable" failures, then the significance of reliability prediction technology is justified.

OBJECTIVES ON THE JOB

The server technician's role in maintaining system integrity is greatly enhanced by utilizing reliability prediction technology. Prevention of unscheduled downtime and data loss is the major benefit of employing this option. By evaluating the performance of certain hardware products, such as hard drives, the server technician is also more informed when making purchase decisions.

PRACTICE TEST QUESTIONS

1. **A lightning strike caused a power surge at Ken's office. Immediately following, the server's disk failure alarm sounded. After stabilizing the system, Ken should document that the hard drive reliability prediction system reported a _____ failure.**
   - a. hot swap
   - b. predictable
   - c. UPS
   - d. nonpredictable

2. **Which of the following options would *not* decrease the incidence of nonpredictable failures of hard drives?**
   - a. improved backup procedures
   - b. improved manufacturing
   - c. improved design process
   - d. improved quality of product

3. **What are the two major types of failures identified by reliability prediction technology?**
   - a. sector/block
   - b. functional/sector
   - c. predictable/nonpredictable
   - d. predictable/electronic

4. **What is the approximate percentage of hard drive failures due to mechanical failure?**
   - a. 15%
   - b. 30%
   - c. 60%
   - d. 75%

5. **What is the major benefit of predicting hard drive failures?**
   - a. prevention of power surges
   - b. prevention of unscheduled downtime and data loss
   - c. the ability to order the proper amount of replacement equipment
   - d. all of the above

6. **How does reliability prediction technology best assist the server technician?**
   - a. gives the technician ample time to perform a backup of data
   - b. allows the technician to repair the hard drive
   - c. prevents downtime and allows time to perform a backup of data before drive failure occurs
   - d. none of the above

7.1 Plan for disaster recovery (continued)

DEVELOP DISASTER RECOVERY PLAN

UNDERSTANDING THE OBJECTIVE

Data and system integrity are the reasons for implementing a disaster recovery plan. This section reviews major areas to consider when devising an effective disaster recovery plan.

WHAT YOU REALLY NEED TO KNOW

- ◆ Analyzing the risk for disaster is the first step in developing a disaster recovery plan.
- ◆ Consideration of what the company can realistically plan to spend on recovery is the next step. Disaster recovery solutions can be quite expensive and should be planned according to a budget that is allowable by corporate standards.
- ◆ Involving upper management in the development of the plan provides you with information about which systems are mission-critical to the organization. Upper management can provide budget and risk assessment information as well.
- ◆ The plan should allow for various outcomes and step-by-step procedures to follow in the event that an option is not successful or applicable.
- ◆ To properly develop a disaster recovery plan, all points of failure must be considered, planned for, and documented.
- ◆ Software redundancy should be documented in great detail, in the event a technician is required to make a decision about accessing offsite data recovery services or performing a backup from tapes stored at an offsite location.
- ◆ Hardware redundancy is addressed with multiple components and a UPS. You should document the plan so that the technician knows what to do first if a failure occurs.
- ◆ Network redundancy also is important. Consider all cables, hubs, and routers as possible points of failure that can have a serious impact on network functionality.
- ◆ In-depth documentation should address hardware, software, the network, and the recovery process itself. Be sure to include important contact information, such as vendor technical support, offsite storage locations, hot-site locations, and so on.
- ◆ Address all changes to the hardware, software, and network in your disaster recovery plan. For instance, adding a new RAID controller could change many steps involved in the original plan.
- ◆ Don't forget the final and most crucial part of the disaster recovery plan: testing. Testing the plan ensures that it is successful in the event of a failure.

OBJECTIVES ON THE JOB

Disaster recovery planning should be performed carefully to ensure its success. After the plan is documented, testing it confirms its functionality. This is not only a skillful method of managing the server environment, but it's cost effective as well.

PRACTICE TEST QUESTIONS

1. **Robert was hired to implement a disaster recovery plan for an existing NT network. What is the first thing Robert should determine?**
   a. type of network in place
   b. risk of failure
   c. type of RAID array in place
   d. UPS requirements

2. **While Robert was implementing the disaster recovery plan for the situation in Question 1, which of the following did he not need to do?**
   a. upgrade all drivers
   b. test the plan
   c. document the plan in detail
   d. determine the budget for the plan

3. **Another technician has installed a new network adapter and a RAID controller in one of the servers on the network for which Robert developed his disaster recovery plan. What should Robert do next?**
   a. update the rest of the drivers
   b. add an additional UPS
   c. update the disaster recovery plan
   d. reconfigure the servers/network

4. **To properly develop a disaster recovery plan, all _____ should be considered.**
   a. updated drivers
   b. error log reports
   c. RAID controller failures
   d. points of failure

5. **Robert is scheduling a meeting to develop a disaster recovery plan. Which of the following personnel should Robert invite to the meeting? (Choose all that apply.)**
   a. department managers
   b. key personnel
   c. data processors
   d. network technicians

6. **What is the main purpose of testing the disaster recovery plan?**
   a. to document its effect on the network
   b. to ensure that the technician onsite knows exactly what to do in the event the plan needs to be used and knows the plan is effective
   c. to ensure the plan is cost effective
   d. to ensure the onsite technician's skills are suitable for your type of server environment

7.1   Plan for disaster recovery (continued)

IDENTIFY TYPES OF BACKUP HARDWARE

UNDERSTANDING THE OBJECTIVE

When choosing the appropriate hardware for backup, you should consider company size, initial setup and maintenance costs, system capabilities, warranty information, backup software, and the server's operating system. You should also consider the capacity, speed, and reliability of the backup hardware when making this important choice. Even with the most elaborate equipment, a backup plan is not reliable unless it is fully tested.

WHAT YOU REALLY NEED TO KNOW

- ◆ For small and medium-sized businesses, backup hardware devices include:
  - Iomega Zip and Jazz drives—Can be SCSI, IDE, or USB; 100 MB, 250 MB, 1 GB, or 2 GB in capacity.
  - CD-R/CD-RW drives—Uses rewriteable CDs; 650 MB per CD.
  - DAT (Digital Audio Tape)—Great for larger systems; inexpensive: DDS-2 (Digital Data Storage) stores 4–8 GB and DDS-3 stores 12–24 GB, both with 4 mm DAT tapes.
  - Travan format tape drives—Slower than DAT; inexpensive; TR-4 stores 4–8 GB, and TR-5 stores 10–20 GB.
- ◆ For larger businesses (with seven or more workstations, any server operating system, or a LAN environment), backup options include Travan and DAT as above and:
  - DLT (Digital Linear Tape) drives and ATLs (Automated Tape Libraries)—The media capacities range from the DLT III, with up to 20 GB capacity, to the DLT IV (with the DLT 8000 tape drive) with up to 80 GB capacity.
  - LTO (Linear Tape Open-Technology) drives—Capable of up to 200 GB compressed data storage.
  - SCSI attached storage options, such as additional hard drive disk enclosures—Attached using RAID technology for redundancy.
  - Fibre Channel options, such as SAN (Storage Area Network)—Enable multiple servers to share a central Fibre Channel RAID storage location.
  - NAS (Network Attached Storage)—Involves direct Ethernet attachment of RAID storage without downtime to existing servers, thereby adding fault tolerance and network bandwidth.

OBJECTIVES ON THE JOB

A server technician's ability to perform a backup routine is an industry standard. Utilizing the most reliable equipment for the company's size and needs enhances your ability to perform this crucial role in a server environment.

PRACTICE TEST QUESTIONS

1. **Steve is managing multiple servers for a large company. He has been given the responsibility of incorporating a viable storage solution. Which of the following is *not* a valid option?**
   a. SAN
   b. Iomega Jazz drive
   c. NAS
   d. ATL

2. **What does NAS stand for?**
   a. Network Attached Storage
   b. Network Automated Service
   c. Novell Automatic Storage
   d. Network Available Storage

3. **Susan has been performing backups for her small company using a DAT drive. While speaking with a co-worker, she learned of another drive called a Travan drive. Which of the two would provide a faster backup for her?**
   a. Both drives are equal in performance.
   b. The Travan drive provides slower backup performance at lower costs.
   c. The DAT drive is faster and capable of storing more data.
   d. The Travan drive provides faster backup than DAT.

4. **Robert is going to purchase a new DLT drive for his company. He wants the ability to store a minimum of 20 GB. Which of the following is *not* an option for his needs?**
   a. TR-4
   b. DLT IV
   c. DLT III
   d. ATL

5. **What type of media is used in a DAT drive?**
   a. digital data storage tapes
   b. digital linear tapes
   c. Travan tapes
   d. Linear Tape Open-Technology tapes

6. **Which storage option enables multiple servers to share a central Fibre Channel RAID storage location?**
   a. NAS
   b. LTO
   c. RAID
   d. SAN

7.1   Plan for disaster recovery (continued)

IDENTIFY TYPES OF BACKUP AND RESTORATION SCHEMES

UNDERSTANDING THE OBJECTIVE

The type of backup scheme performed depends on the following factors: backup hardware, server operating system, cost, and the needs of the business. Another very important factor to consider is the type of data you will be replicating.

WHAT YOU REALLY NEED TO KNOW

◆ Types of backups:
  - Full—Usually performed weekly and involves a complete replication of all data chosen for backup.
  - Differential—Usually performed daily after a full backup and involves a replication of data that has changed since the last full backup.
  - Incremental—Usually performed daily after a full backup and involves a replication of data that has changed since the last full backup. Each subsequent incremental backup performed only replicates the data that has changed since the last incremental. Therefore, incremental backups are faster than differentials due to the amount of data being replicated. However, restoring data that was backed up incrementally is slower because data from the last full backup plus data from all other incrementals are needed for full restoration.

◆ There are many software vendors that provide advanced options for performing backup schemes. For example:
  - Native Operating System Backup Utilities
  - Cheyenne ArcServe
  - Veritas Backup Exec

◆ A sample backup scheme is as follows:
  - Weekly—Perform a full backup of all data needed in the event of data loss. Verify that the data has been replicated successfully.
  - Daily—Perform an incremental backup of the data that has changed since the last full backup. Verify that the data has been replicated.

◆ It is standard practice to store backups offsite in the event that damage occurs onsite. This is a very important step in assuring that the backups you have performed are useful in the event of data loss.

OBJECTIVES ON THE JOB

A server technician's responsibility to perform a backup routine is an industry standard. The backup routine determines the reliability of your data recovery/restoration process. Verifying all backup procedures as well as the data itself is highly recommended.

PRACTICE TEST QUESTIONS

1. **John is in the process of developing a backup scheme for his 10-user NT network. Which of the following is a viable backup option?**
   a. using the backup utility provided with NT
   b. performing a full backup daily
   c. using offsite storage
   d. all of the above

2. **Brenda has been performing backups regularly for one month. Her routine is a weekly full backup of all data and a daily differential backup. What is required for a full restoration of data in the event of data loss?**
   a. only the full backup tape for that week
   b. the last full backup and all differential tapes for that week
   c. only the differential tapes for that week
   d. all of the differential tapes ever replicated

3. **When should a differential backup be performed?**
   a. daily, after a weekly full backup is performed
   b. weekly, after a daily full backup is performed
   c. daily, after a weekly incremental backup is performed
   d. weekly, after a daily incremental backup is performed

4. **Which of the following backup strategies provides the fastest recovery procedure in the event of data loss?**
   a. differential
   b. incremental
   c. full
   d. partial

5. **What is the most common method of ensuring access to data in the event of a natural disaster onsite and loss of all local data?**
   a. locked closet for tape storage onsite
   b. network backup scheme
   c. offsite tape storage
   d. none of the above

6. **What should you do to verify the data replicated in the event that you need to perform data restoration?**
   a. Verify the full backup data that is replicated weekly.
   b. Verify the differential backup data daily only.
   c. Verify that the data has been replicated after each backup is performed.
   d. Verify the incremental backup data only.

7. **What are the three major types of backup schemes used today?**
   a. replicated, full, and weekly
   b. offsite, local, and incremental
   c. verified, partial, and incremental
   d. full, incremental, and differential

7.1   Plan for disaster recovery (continued)

IDENTIFY TYPES OF BACKUP AND RESTORATION SCHEMES (CONTINUED)

UNDERSTANDING THE OBJECTIVE

Data loss can be caused by any number of events—for instance, natural disasters, hardware failures, software corruption, and human error. A good backup plan is fortified by its method of restoration. These methods can vary greatly depending on the platform used for backing up data. Often, due to hardware failure or software corruption, original data becomes unavailable. In this instance, recovery of the original data may be required.

WHAT YOU REALLY NEED TO KNOW

◆ The difference between recovery and restoration can be defined as follows: If lost data can be retrieved from damaged media or files, it involves recovery. If lost data can be replaced with data that has been stored offsite or on backup media, it involves restoration.

◆ Often, it is necessary to boot from a specific boot diskette to begin the restoration process. Then, the technician should load the appropriate media to restore the lost data.

◆ If damage or corruption to hardware or files has occurred, there are various solutions available to help you retrieve your data. Third-party software is available as well as service providers that specialize in the retrieval of data, often without damage to the hardware involved.

◆ Check with your hardware manufacturer regarding the warranty violation policy if recovery of data involves opening the device.

◆ Third-party data recovery and restoration software offers fast and reliable options for recovery in the event that there is a large amount of data to be restored. For example, Cheyenne ArcServe provides the following methods for locating the files needed for restoration:

 - Restoring by tree—Using its database, the software reconstructs a directory tree in the browser of all machines, directories, and files that were backed up.

 - Restoring by tape—Using its database, the software displays all tapes used for backups and the source for each session on the tape.

 - Restoring by query—You specify a search pattern and the software locates the specified files within its stored database.

 - Restoring by tape media—Data is restored from the entire tape used for that backup session.

OBJECTIVES ON THE JOB

Incorporate methods to recover and restore data into your backup plan. Providing your company with the support needed to prevent or minimize downtime and loss of revenue is essential.

PRACTICE TEST QUESTIONS

1. **Bob arrived to find that one of the servers he routinely supports has a failed hard drive. The data from the drive has not been backed up since last week, because backups are only performed weekly in this facility. The server will not reboot into the operating system. What is the *best* solution to ensure a full restoration of data?**
   a. Install a new hard drive and restore the data from the last full backup.
   b. Employ the recovery portion of his company's backup plan to recover the current data from the damaged hard drive and restore from that data.
   c. Boot with the emergency boot diskette and restore from media.
   d. none of the above

2. **In the event that data is lost without damage to hardware/files on the server, which of the following is necessary?**
   a. Employ the restoration portion of the company's backup plan.
   b. Restore with the last full backup tape for that week.
   c. Employ the recovery portion of the company's backup plan to recover the current data from the damaged hard drive and restore from that data.
   d. Install a new hard drive and restore the data from the last full backup.

3. **Susan will be shipping a set of hard drives offsite for data recovery. Which of the following steps should she take to ensure that the drives would still be replaced if they are under warranty?**
   a. Advise the data recovery service provider not to open the drive casings.
   b. No action is necessary, as the drives most likely will not need to be replaced.
   c. Contact the hard drive manufacturer to check the violation-of-warranty policy when data loss has occurred.
   d. Susan should not send the drives to a service provider, as this will automatically violate the warranty of all devices.

4. **Which of the following is *not* a restoration method?**
   a. by tree
   b. by incremental backup
   c. by query
   d. by media

5. **What is the main purpose of incorporating a method for restoring data into your company's backup plan?**
   a. to retrieve data lost due to damage to hardware or corruption of files
   b. to minimize the amount of backups performed during the week
   c. to replace data that has been lost with data that has been stored on backup media or offsite
   d. to provide the technician with the choice of retrieving data from tape media or from offsite sources

7.1 Plan for disaster recovery (continued)

CONFIRM AND USE OFF SITE STORAGE FOR BACKUP

UNDERSTANDING THE OBJECTIVE

Establishing an offsite storage protocol is one of the best ways to ensure that data can be recovered when a disaster occurs. You must understand the importance of offsite storage and the processes involved in implementing a successful offsite plan in order to utilize this option for backing up your company's data.

WHAT YOU REALLY NEED TO KNOW

- ◆ Offsite storage consists of storing backups at a location that is some distance from the main site. This ensures that if a disaster (such as fire, tornado, or flood) occurs, the organization's data can be retrieved and restored to a server.

- ◆ Depending on your backup strategy, tapes should be rotated to offsite storage on a regular basis to ensure that you have the most current data offsite. Some organizations store data offsite for considerable amounts of time. When doing so, consider the life expectancy of the media. Backup tapes degrade after being offsite for long periods of time, rendering backup tapes useless. If it is necessary for you to store data for long periods of time, consider media that is capable of meeting those requirements.

- ◆ Ensure that your offsite storage media is placed in a secure location. Media should be placed in a locked location with restricted access. You should also ensure that media is kept away from hazards (such as fluorescent lights, heat, and humidity) that could damage or destroy your backups. Most organizations place media in a fireproof safe to prevent damage.

- ◆ Always maintain inventory and documentation (hard copy and soft copy) of offsite storage. A copy of the documentation should be included with your offsite storage media.

- ◆ Always maintain a copy of your organization's backup software offsite. In the event of a disaster, you must have a way to restore data to the server. Backup software packages are different and may not be able to recognize a backup that was created using another software package. Keeping a copy of backup software offsite can save a considerable amount of time.

OBJECTIVES ON THE JOB

Offsite storage is vital to an organization's well being. You must always perform the offsite storage procedures mandated by your organization. Doing so ensures that when a disaster strikes, your organization has the ability to recover in a timely manner. Review your organization's offsite storage policy and consider ways to improve offsite procedures.

PRACTICE TEST QUESTIONS

1. **Which of the following items should accompany your offsite media? (Choose all that apply.)**
   a. documentation
   b. extra tapes
   c. backup software
   d. tape degasser

2. **Which of the following is the best location for offsite storage?**
   a. the main building's computer room
   b. downstairs in the same building
   c. across the street
   d. several blocks away at a second company site

3. **While performing inventory, Sara discovers outdated tapes in offsite storage. What should Sara do? (Choose all that apply.)**
   a. Document changes to inventory.
   b. Do nothing.
   c. Erase the tapes.
   d. Replace the outdated tapes with current tapes.

4. **Which of the following provides the best protection for offsite media?**
   a. plastic bag
   b. taped box
   c. fireproof safe
   d. tape rack

5. **Which of the following can cause damage to offsite media? (Choose all that apply.)**
   a. time
   b. heat
   c. humidity
   d. users

7.1 Plan for disaster recovery (continued)

DOCUMENT AND TEST DISASTER RECOVERY PLAN REGULARLY, AND UPDATE AS NEEDED

UNDERSTANDING THE OBJECTIVE

When creating a disaster recovery plan for your server environment, it is important to document, test, and update your recovery plan as required.

WHAT YOU REALLY NEED TO KNOW

- ◆ There are many processes that must be performed in a server environment, all of which must be documented thoroughly in your disaster recovery plan.
- ◆ When documenting a disaster recovery plan, ensure that the following items are included in your documentation:
  - All key members (including primary and secondary persons in charge) of the disaster recovery team and their contact information
  - An updated inventory of all hardware and software in the server environment
  - Vendor contact information for all server hardware and software
  - Standard operating procedures of recovery processes for specific disasters
- ◆ Testing a disaster recovery plan is the best way to ensure that your plan meets the requirements of your organization. Information received from testing can be used to highlight weaknesses in an organization's disaster recovery plan and assist you with improving the plan. You should create scenarios that test different aspects of a disaster recovery plan and test your plan regularly. Information gathered from the scenario should be documented and compared to previous evolutions.
- ◆ Technology is advancing faster now than ever before. Organizations are constantly replacing hardware and software with products that increase their productivity. This is why it is very important to update your disaster recovery plan when necessary. Replacement or modification of servers, network topologies, and software are all reasons to modify your disaster recovery plan.
- ◆ When upgrading server hardware or software, it is important to ensure that your procedures are updated in your disaster recovery plan as well. Procedures for a new server may be entirely different than the procedures for your previous server.

OBJECTIVES ON THE JOB

When a disaster strikes, an organization must rely on its disaster recovery plan to successfully recover from the disaster. Always ensure that your prepared plan serves its purpose. You can ensure this by testing and updating your plan when appropriate.

PRACTICE TEST QUESTIONS

1. **Testing a disaster recovery plan will do which of the following? (Choose all that apply.)**
   a. ensure that the plan meets organizational requirements
   b. upset upper management
   c. waste time
   d. highlight problems with the plan

2. **Which of the following should be documented in a disaster recovery plan? (Choose all that apply.)**
   a. members of the disaster recovery team
   b. server price guide
   c. updated inventory of all servers
   d. vendor information

3. **XYZ Corporation just performed a major upgrade. All NetWare servers were migrated to new servers running Windows 2000, and the Token Ring network was replaced with an Ethernet-based network. Which aspects of the disaster recovery plan should be updated?**
   a. servers and software only
   b. servers, network, and software
   c. network and software only
   d. servers and network only

4. **Jason just installed a new RAID controller in his server. The new controller uses a different procedure for creating an array. What should Jason do? (Choose all that apply.)**
   a. Update the hardware section of his disaster recovery plan.
   b. Do nothing.
   c. Store the documentation on the shelf.
   d. Update the RAID controller procedures in his disaster recovery plan.

5. **A disaster recovery plan should provide _____ information about your organization.**
   a. brief
   b. some
   c. encrypted
   d. detailed

7.2   Restoring

IDENTIFY HARDWARE REPLACEMENTS • IDENTIFY HOT AND COLD SITES

UNDERSTANDING THE OBJECTIVE

Hardware replacement is a critical factor in restoring an organization's server. Organizations apply different processes of restoration depending on the severity of the disaster. Be familiar with hardware replacement procedures and hot and cold sites.

WHAT YOU REALLY NEED TO KNOW

◆ A **hot site** is a facility designated by an organization to handle all operations if its primary site fails. A hot site is fully operational and has all the hardware and software (including backups and company data) that the primary site contains. A properly designed hot site can provide an almost transparent changeover of operations when a disaster occurs.

◆ A **cold site** is a facility designated to handle operations when a disaster occurs. Unlike a hot site, a cold site is a space that has to be equipped with all the necessary hardware and software to resume operations. When selecting a cold site, ensure that it meets your organization's requirements.

◆ When defective hardware brings a server down, it is important to replace that hardware as soon as possible. Documentation of all your server components and their settings should be available to perform this hardware replacement more quickly. In addition, most organizations keep additional components on hand to ensure that components can be quickly replaced if a failure occurs.

◆ It is important to establish a solid relationship with your hardware vendors. Vendors can provide you with information about available options for your server and hardware.

◆ Ensure that you have the appropriate contract for your server. Server vendors offer contracts ranging from next-day service to two-hour service. You must consider how vital the server is to the organization when purchasing a service agreement. Having the wrong type of service contract can cost an organization a considerable amount of time and money. Your server vendor can provide you with information about the appropriate agreement for your server.

◆ Many organizations cannot afford for servers to be down for long periods of time. When a disaster occurs, the organization must recover quickly or risk losing millions of dollars. Depending on how critical operations are, organizations use a hot site or cold site for recovery.

OBJECTIVES ON THE JOB

Organizations rely heavily on their technicians for solutions when disasters occur. By carefully planning procedures, identifying replacement hardware, and choosing the correct recovery method, you ensure that your organization can quickly recover and resume normal operations.

PRACTICE TEST QUESTIONS

1. **Which of the following is true about a cold site? (Choose all that apply.)**
   a. It has no hardware installed.
   b. It is only a designated space.
   c. It has systems online.
   d. It already has a network in place.

2. **XYZ Corporation loses $1 million every hour its servers are down. Which of the following is the best method of disaster recovery for XYZ?**
   a. storing replacement hard drives
   b. a hot site
   c. a cold site
   d. none of the above

3. **Which of the following is true about a hot site? (Choose all that apply.)**
   a. It is a fully operational site.
   b. It has the same hardware as the primary site.
   c. It has no hardware on location.
   d. It can provide an almost transparent changeover of operations.

4. **Bill will be purchasing a mission-critical server for his company. Which of the following is true?**
   a. Bill needs to purchase additional servers for backup.
   b. No service agreement is needed.
   c. Bill should speak with the manufacturer to determine the best option.
   d. none of the above

5. **Tom is purchasing a new server. Which of the following will assist Tom with disaster recovery? (Choose all that apply.)**
   a. an additional hard drive for a spare
   b. additional client licenses for NT
   c. the appropriate service contract
   d. a rack-mounted server

6. **When using a cold site instead of a hot site, the recovery process will _____**
   a. take the least amount of time
   b. take a greater amount of time
   c. take the same amount of time
   d. make the recovery transparent

7.2 Restoring (continued)

IMPLEMENT DISASTER RECOVERY PLAN

UNDERSTANDING THE OBJECTIVE

When a problem is identified as a potential threat to an organization, a disaster plan can reduce or eliminate the possibility of that threat. Therefore, you must understand the process of implementing a disaster recovery plan.

WHAT YOU REALLY NEED TO KNOW

◆ Before implementing a disaster recovery plan, ensure that the plan has been thoroughly reviewed and documented. The plan must meet your organization's needs if it is to be successful.

◆ Management plays a key role in the disaster recovery plan. The plan should be distributed to all departments within an organization and reviewed with all employees. Involving upper management ensures that the plan is taken seriously and enforced at all levels of an organization.

◆ Training is one of the keys to a disaster recovery plan. Some aspects of the plan may require specific training for personnel. Training personnel provides you with people who are able to quickly identify and resolve problems related to a disaster.

◆ You must determine which areas of a disaster recovery plan should be implemented first. The disaster recovery plan may be implemented in phases, due to budget restrictions within an organization. By prioritizing your implementation, you can ensure that issues that require immediate attention are addressed first.

◆ Implementation of the disaster recovery plan should be documented and updated as required. In the process of implementing the plan, you may discover other areas that the organization needs to address. By documenting your implementation, you ensure that you have information that can be used to enhance your plan.

◆ After your disaster recovery plan has been finalized, you must test your plan on a regular basis. Every disaster situation is unique and requires a different approach for recovery. By using different scenarios, you are able to evaluate how an organization responds to different types of disasters. Information obtained from testing can be used to track the progress of your organization.

OBJECTIVES ON THE JOB

Implementing a disaster recovery plan helps to resolve many problems before they occur. When a disaster strikes, proper implementation ensures that you have trained personnel and available resources to handle the incident.

PRACTICE TEST QUESTIONS

1. **Which of the following should be performed before implementing a disaster recovery plan? (Choose all that apply.)**
   a. documentation
   b. testing
   c. a thorough review
   d. printing

2. **Which of the following disaster recovery resolutions should be implemented first?**
   a. backup strategy for the PDC
   b. establishing a cold site
   c. moving servers to a remote location
   d. specialized training for personnel

3. **When implementing and testing a disaster recovery plan, testing regularly using different scenarios provides which of the following? (Choose all that apply.)**
   a. ability to obtain information that can be used to track the progress of your organization
   b. ability to evaluate how an organization responds to different types of disasters
   c. ability to resolve problems before they occur
   d. ability to provide trained personnel to handle problems

4. **Which of the following is responsible for disaster recovery?**
   a. CEO
   b. project manager
   c. facilities manager
   d. everyone

5. **Involving upper management in disaster recovery assists you in which of the following? (Choose all that apply.)**
   a. implementing the plan across all departments
   b. upsetting employees
   c. enforcing the plan
   d. cutting corners on the plan

6. **Trained personnel play a key role in disaster recovery. Why is it important to review the disaster recovery plan?**
   a. because trained personnel are important to a successful disaster recovery plan
   b. to be able to replace parts as needed
   c. to locate the system specifications
   d. to find the latest update procedures for drivers

Answer Key for Practice Questions

Section 1.0
Objective 1.1
Practice Questions:

    1. c
    2. c
    3. d
    4. b
    5. a
    6. a

Objective 1.1 (continued)
Practice Questions:

    1. c
    2. b
    3. a
    4. d
    5. d

Objective 1.1 (continued)
Practice Questions:

    1. b
    2. d
    3. c
    4. d
    5. a
    6. c

Objective 1.2
Practice Questions:

    1. b
    2. d
    3. a
    4. b
    5. b
    6. a

Objective 1.2 (continued)
Practice Questions:

    1. a
    2. b
    3. b
    4. d
    5. c
    6. a

Objective 1.2 (continued)
Practice Questions:
1. a
2. b
3. c
4. b
5. d
6. b

Objective 1.2 (continued)
Practice Questions:
1. a
2. d
3. b
4. d
5. d
6. a

Objective 1.2 (continued)
Practice Questions:
1. c
2. b
3. d
4. a
5. d
6. a

Objective 1.2 (continued)
Practice Questions:
1. d
2. a
3. b
4. a
5. d
6. b

Section 2.0

Objective 2.1

Practice Questions:

1. a,b,c,d
2. a
3. a, c
4. c
5. d
6. c

Objective 2.1 (continued)

Practice Questions:

1. c
2. a
3. b, c
4. b, c
5. c
6. b

Objective 2.2

Practice Questions:

1. b
2. d
3. a
4. b
5. b

Objective 2.2 (continued)

Practice Questions:

1. b
2. b
3. c
4. d
5. b
6. c

Objective 2.3

Practice Questions:

1. b
2. a
3. c
4. d
5. b
6. d

Objective 2.3 (continued)
Practice Questions:
1. b
2. c
3. a
4. c
5. d
6. b

Objective 2.4
Practice Questions:
1. c
2. b
3. c
4. a
5. b
6. b

Objective 2.5
Practice Questions:
1. d
2. a
3. d
4. b
5. c
6. b

Objective 2.6
Practice Questions:
1. c
2. a
3. b
4. b
5. d
6. a

Objective 2.7
Practice Questions:
1. b
2. d
3. d
4. b
5. d
6. c
7. a

Objective 2.7 (continued)

Practice Questions:

1. d
2. d
3. d
4. b
5. a
6. a

Objective 2.8

Practice Questions:

1. d
2. a
3. c
4. d
5. d
6. a

Objective 2.9

Practice Questions:

1. a
2. c
3. d
4. b
5. a

Section 3.0

Objective 3.1

Practice Questions:

1. c
2. d
3. a
4. d
5. a,c
6. a,c
7. b

Objective 3.2

Practice Questions:

1. c
2. b
3. c
4. b,c
5. a,b
6. d

Objective 3.2 (continued)

Practice Questions:

1. a
2. d
3. a,c
4. b
5. b

Objective 3.2 (continued)

Practice Questions:

1. c
2. b,c
3. c
4. a
5. d
6. b

Objective 3.3

Practice Questions:

1. b,c,d
2. b
3. a,b,c
4. b,c
5. a
6. d

Objective 3.3 (continued)
Practice Questions:
1. a
2. c
3. b
4. d
5. c

Objective 3.3 (continued)
Practice Questions:
1. a
2. b
3. b
4. c
5. d

Objective 3.4
Practice Questions:
1. d
2. a
3. c
4. d
5. c
6. d

Objective 3.5
Practice Questions:
1. a,b,c
2. a,b
3. b
4. c
5. a,c
6. a,b,c

Objective 3.6
Practice Questions:
1. b
2. a,b,c
3. c
4. d
5. a
6. c
7. a,b,d

Objective 3.7
Practice Questions:
1. c
2. a,b,c,d
3. b,c,d
4. a,b,d
5. a,b,d
6. b

Objective 3.8
Practice Questions:
1. b
2. d
3. a
4. b
5. b
6. d
7. a,b

Objective 3.9
Practice Questions:
1. a
2. b,d
3. b
4. c
5. a,b,d
6. c
7. d

Objective 3.10
Practice Questions:
1. d
2. a,b,d
3. c
4. d
5. c
6. d
7. d

Section 4.0

Objective 4.1

Practice Questions:

1. c
2. b
3. b
4. c
5. a
6. a,b,d
7. d

Objective 4.2

Practice Questions:

1. a,c,d
2. a,b,c,d
3. b
4. a
5. c
6. a
7. c

Objective 4.3

Practice Questions:

1. c
2. a
3. b
4. b
5. c
6. b
7. d

Objective 4.4

Practice Questions:

1. b,c,d
2. a,b,c,d
3. a
4. b
5. b,d
6. a,b,d
7. d

Objective 4.5
Practice Questions:
1. a,b,d
2. a,c
3. a,b,d
4. d
5. a,c,d
6. a,c
7. d

Objective 4.6
Practice Questions:
1. a,b,c,d
2. c
3. b
4. a,b
5. a,c
6. a.b.d
7. c

Section 5.0

Objective 5.1

Practice Questions:

1. a,c
2. a,b,d
3. c
4. c
5. a,b,c
6. a,c
7. d

Objective 5.2

Practice Questions:

1. d
2. a,b,c,d
3. a,b,c
4. c
5. b,c
6. b
7. b

Section 6.0

Objective 6.1

Practice Questions:

1. a,b,c,d
2. a,b,c
3. d
4. a
5. a,d
6. a

Objective 6.2

Practice Questions:

1. b,c
2. c
3. b
4. b
5. b
6. b
7. b

Objective 6.2 (continued)

Practice Questions:

1. a
2. b,c
3. b
4. d
5. a
6. a,c
7. b

Objective 6.2 (continued)

Practice Questions:

1. b
2. c
3. b
4. d
5. b
6. a,b,c,d
7. b

Objective 6.2 (continued)
Practice Questions:
1. a,b
2. d
3. a
4. c
5. c
6. d
7. a

Objective 6.2 (continued)
Practice Questions:
1. b
2. c
3. b
4. d
5. a,d
6. c
7. d

Objective 6.2 (continued)
Practice Questions:
1. d
2. b
3. a,b,c,d
4. a,d
5. a,b,d
6. a,c
7. d

Objective 6.2 (continued)
Practice Questions:
1. a,b,d
2. b
3. b,d
4. b,c
5. b
6. c
7. d

Objective 6.2 (continued)
Practice Questions:
1. b
2. a,b,c
3. c
4. b
5. a,b
6. a,b,d

Objective 6.2 (continued)
Practice Questions:
1. a,d
2. a
3. a,c
4. a,b,d
5. c
6. a,b,c
7. d

Objective 6.2 (continued)
Practice Questions:
1. b
2. c
3. a,b,d
4. a,b
5. c
6. a,b,c,d

Objective 6.2 (continued)
Practice Questions:
1. a,b,c,d
2. a,c,d
3. c
4. d
5. a,c
6. b,c

Objective 6.2 (continued)
Practice Questions:
1. b
2. a,b,d
3. b
4. c
5. c
6. a,b,c.d
7. b,c,d

Objective 6.2 (continued)
Practice Questions:
1. a,b,c,d
2. a,b,c
3. c
4. a,c
5. a,b,c
6. c

Objective 6.3

Practice Questions:

1. b,d
2. b
3. a,c,d
4. a,b,d
5. b
6. a,c
7. d

Objective 6.4

Practice Questions:

1. a,b,c
2. c
3. b
4. b,d
5. a,b
6. c
7. b,d

Objective 6.5

Practice Questions:

1. a,b,d
2. a,b,c
3. b
4. a,c
5. c
6. a
7. b,c

Section 7.0

Objective 7.1

Practice Questions:

    1. c
    2. b
    3. a
    4. c
    5. d

Objective 7.1 (continued)

Practice Questions:

    1. d
    2. a
    3. d
    4. a
    5. c
    6. d

Objective 7.1 (continued)

Practice Questions:

    1. b
    2. a
    3. d
    4. c
    5. b
    6. c

Objective 7.1 (continued)

Practice Questions:

    1. d
    2. a
    3. c
    4. c
    5. b
    6. c

Objective 7.1 (continued)

Practice Questions:

    1. b
    2. a
    3. c
    4. d
    5. a, b
    6. b

Objective 7.1 (continued)

Practice Questions:

1. b
2. a
3. c
4. a
5. a
6. d

Objective 7.1 (continued)

Practice Questions:

1. d
2. b
3. a
4. a
5. c
6. c
7. d

Objective 7.1 (continued)

Practice Questions:

1. b
2. a
3. c
4. b
5. c

Objective 7.1 (continued)

Practice Questions:

1. a, c
2. d
3. a, d
4. c
5. a, b, c, d

Objective 7.1 (continued)

Practice Questions:

1. a, d
2. a, c, d
3. b
4. a, d
5. d

Objective 7.2

Practice Questions:

1. a, b
2. b
3. a, b, d
4. a
5. a, c
6. b

Objective 7.2 (continued)

Practice Questions:

1. a, c
2. a
3. a, b, c, d
4. d
5. a, c
6. a

GLOSSARY

A

agent — A network-management software module that resides in a managed device.

AT Attachment/Integrated Drive Electronics (ATA/IDE) — Hard drive implementation that has the controller on the hard disk drive.

B

baseline — A collection of data that establishes acceptable performance. You compare variances in performance against the baseline to determine whether perceived performance issues are real.

Basic Input/Output System (BIOS) — A series of input and output configuration settings for peripherals, adapters, and on-board components.

benchmark — A test used to compare performance of hardware or software on a server.

brownouts — Low voltage in power lines causing lights to dim or flicker.

C

cable management arm (CMA) — Rack equipment that allows orderly arrangement of cables, and expands and contracts so that you can move equipment on the rack without accidentally unplugging it.

Category 5 cable — Most common type of twisted-pair cable used in Ethernet networks.

CD-ROM — A peripheral device that reads information from compact discs.

central processing unit (CPU) — Most important component of the server. Most calculations are processed in the CPU, the brains of the server.

CMOS — Complimentary metal oxide semiconductor that includes a small amount of memory, the purpose of which is to store the BIOS settings.

coaxial — Type of cable used for wiring networks. Cable used by the 10Base2 system of Ethernet.

cold site — A disaster recovery facility designed to receive computer equipment. All power, water, air conditioning, raised floor, and other items requiring a long lead-time to aquire, install, and house a computer center are in place.

communications (COM) port — Used for connecting peripheral devices to the server.

compact disc (CD) — A disc made of polycarbonate and one or more layers of metal. Used to store information.

crimping — The process of attaching a connector to a cable using the required tool.

cyper locks — A special type of lock that requires a unique code (usually a combination of numbers) for a person to gain entry to the room.

D

Desktop Management Interface (DMI) — Similar to SNMP, except that it contains specific information about an actual device.

diagonal cutters — Cutting tool most commonly used to cut flat ribbon cable.

differential backups — Backs up files that have changed since the last full backup.

E

electromagnetic interference (EMI) — A low-voltage, low-current, high-frequency signal that interferes with normal network transmission.

(EIA/TIA) Electronic Industries Association/ Telecommunications Industries Association — Organization that defines electronics standards in the United States.

electrostatic discharge (ESD) — A discharge of electrical energy that occurs when two objects with differing electrical potential come into contact with one another because the electrical charges seek to equalize.

emergency repair disks (ERDs) — Disks that are created for a Windows NT server to assist with recovery of a software failure.

Extended Industry Standard Architecture (EISA) — An evolution of ISA, the EISA bus provides backward compatibility with older ISA devices and provides maximum bus bandwidth of about 33 MBps.

F

fault tolerance — Continued service despite failure of a server or component.

fiber optic cable — Technology that uses glass (or plastic) threads (fibers) to transmit data using light pulses. The receiving end of the message converts the light signal to binary values. The maximum length is 25 km (15.5 miles) with speeds up to 2 Gbps.

field replaceable unit (FRU) — A system with replaceable CPU, CMOS, CMOS battery, RAM, and RAM cache.

firmware — Software located in the read-only memory of a device.

(FAQ) frequently asked question — List published by companies that provides answers to common questions or issues about a product or service.

full backup — A complete backup of all files located on a server.

G

gigabyte (GB) — Unit of information storage equal to 1,073,741,824 bytes.

H

Hardware Compatibility List (HCL) — A list that displays all compatible hardware for an operating system.

hot fix — A NetWare feature that verifies the integrity of all disk writes. If a write fails this verification, the data is redirected to a hot fix area and the original destination is marked as unusable. The default size of the hot fix area is a small percentage of a partition's total size.

hot site — A location containing computers and necessary peripheral equipment that may be occupied or utilized by a subscriber immediately after a disaster declaration to restore its own systems, applications, and data.

hub — A network device that connects network cables together in a central, star configuration. Passive hubs simply make the connections; active hubs (multiport repeaters) regenerate the signal to increase the distance it can travel.

I

incremental backup — A backup of only those files that have been created or changed since the last normal or incremental backup, which can reduce the amount of time that is required to complete the backup process. It marks files as having been backed up by setting the archive bit.

Input/Output (I/O) — The process of data entering and leaving a computer.

Integrated Drive Electronics (IDE) — Refers to any hard disk with an integrated controller. Closely associated with the ATA standard.

Internet Protocol (IP) — The network layer protocol upon which the Internet is based.

Internetwork Packet Exchange (IPX) — A networking protocol used by NetWare operating systems.

Interrupt Request (IRQ) — An electrical signal that obtains the CPU's attention in order to handle an event immediately, although the processor might queue the request behind other requests.

K

keyboard, video, mouse (KVM) switch — Enables you to use a single keyboard, monitor and mouse for several servers.

L

light-emitting diode (LED) — A diode that emits light when current is passed through it.
local area network (LAN) — A collection of computers in close proximity to one another on a single network.

M

Management Information Base (MIB) — A database of definitions for the specific SNMP device being monitored.
Master/Slave/Cable Select (MA/SL/CS) — Jumper settings that are common for ATA/IDE drives.
mean time between failures (MTBF) — The anticipated lifetime of a computer or its components.
megabyte (MB) — Unit of information storage equal to 1,048,576 bytes.
megahertz (MHz) — Unit of measurement for indicating frequency of one million cycles per second.
Microsoft Disk Operating System (MS DOS) — A collection of programs developed by Microsoft that enable a user to manage information and hardware on a computer.
modular crimp tool — Common tool used to attach RJ-11/12/45 plugs to twisted-pair cable.

N

Nbstat — Utility that displays NetBIOS over TCP/IP statistics.

NetBIOS — Broadcast-based name resolution scheme where a client simply broadcasts the NetBIOS name of the computer it wishes to reach to all of the computers in a subnet. The broadcast message identifies a computer that acknowledges the broadcast and establishes a communication link.
Netstat — Utility display status and state of TCP/IP connections.
Network Interface Card (NIC) — The workstation's adapter card that connects to the network and through which network communications take place.
(NOS) network operating system — Provides file and printer sharing, centralized file storage, security, and various services. Primary examples of a NOS include Microsoft Windows NT or 2000, Linux, IBM OS/2, and Novell NetWare.

O

operating system (OS) — A collection of programs used for computer operation that accept and interpret information and perform input and output procedures between the computer and all devices.

P

packet identifiers (PIDs) — Information at the beginning of a packet about the host and destination computer.
Packet Internet Groper (PING) — Utility used to verify connectivity between two TCP/IP hosts.
Peripheral Component Interconnect/ Industry Standard Architecture (PCI/ISA) — A local bus standard developed by IBM. Common bus speeds are 32 bit and 64 bit.

Power Distribution Units (PDUs) — Provide clean power for rack-mounted servers and provide protection from power spikes and surges.

Power-On Self-Test (POST) — Verifies functionality of motherboard hardware.

R

rack — A cabinet that houses stacked network equipment, storage, and servers. A rack can store multiple items in the same floor space.

Random Access Memory (RAM) — Most common memory found in a computer. Memory that is randomly accessed by the computer.

redundancy — The ability to continue providing service when something fails. For example, if a hard disk fails, a redundant hard disk can continue to store and serve files.

Redundant Array of Inexpensive (or Independent) Disks (RAID) — Utilization of multiple disks to improve performance, provide redundancy, or both.

Registered Jack-45 (RJ-45) — An eight-wire connector for Ethernet network devices.

remote alerts — An alert sent from a computer or server that is not attached to a workstation.

revolutions per minute (RPM) — Reference used for hard disk speed.

S

(SCA) single connector attachment — Disk drive connector that has power and data cable connections. Used with SCSI drives.

self-monitoring, analysis, and reporting technology (SMART) — Technology that monitors the health of hard drives in a server and reports potential problems.

Simple Network Management Protocol (SNMP) — A network monitoring and management protocol. Its usefulness is comprised of several elements that work together with the ultimate purpose of informing the administrator of a changing trend in the use of an object or alerting the administrator of an error, failure, or condition.

Small Computer System Interface (SCSI) — An ANSI standard used for attaching peripheral devices to a computer.

SNMP trap — A message sent by the agent when a specified condition is met or exceeded.

storage area network (SAN) — generally refers to Fibre Channel and any other type of network-based storage solution that is not server-based.

striping — The process of writing data across multiple hard drives.

System Setup Utility (SSU) — An important tool that varies depending on the manufacturer. It can perform the following types of functions: assigning resources to devices/expansion cards, setting boot device order and system security options, viewing and clearing the system event log, and viewing the system field-replaceable units (FRUs) and sensor data records (SDRs). It also allows troubleshooting of the server when the operating system is not functioning. A downloadable version of the server's SSU is usually available on the manufacturer's Web site.

T

threshold — A specific setting for a managed device.

Tracert — Utility that traces a packet from the computer to the Internet host.

Transmission Control Protocol/Internet Protocol (TCP/IP) — A suite of protocols in use on most networks and the Internet.

U

Uniform Resource Locators (URLs) — The global address for resources and documents on the World Wide Web.

Uninterruptible Power Supply (UPS) — A device that supplies power to allow administrators to perform a graceful shutdown of server equipment. Otherwise, the sudden loss of power to the server can be extremely damaging to the operating system, applications, and open data files.

Unit of Measure (U) — Used to reference the amount of space used by a rack-mounted server.

Universal Serial Bus (USB) — An external bus standard that supports transfer rates up to 12 Mbps and can have up to 127 devices attached.

universal stripping tool — Tool used for stripping different types of wire.

W

wake-on LAN (WOL) — A technology that allows you to remotely wake a computer from sleep mode. WOL works by sending a "magic packet" from a remote station to the WOL host. The "magic packet" contains 16 copies of the WOL host's MAC address.

wide area network (WAN) — Multiple, geographically distant LANs connected to one another across a relatively great distance.

Wired for Management (WfM) — Open industry specification developed by IBM for managing a computer over a network.

INDEX

A

adapters, 64, 118
  moving to different slot, 104
  NO POST NO VIDEO
    problems, 122
Agent accelerators, 38
agents, 68
alerts
  controllers, 18
  messages, 116
anti-static packaging, 16
anti-tip plate, 8
anti-virus software, 122
application logs, 40, 92
applications
  incompatible, 122
  information about, 92
ATA/IDE (AT Attachment/ Integrated Drive
  Electronics) hard drives, 56
ATLs (Automated Tape Libraries), 134

B

backup and recovery schemes, 136–139
Backup Exec, 38
backup hardware, 134
backup server, 2
backup software, 38, 46
backups
  current, 34
  daily, 136
  differential, 46, 74, 136
  full, 46, 58, 74, 136
  incremental, 46, 74, 136
  offsite storage, 138
  regular, 74
  remote servers, 38
  security, 86
  specific time for, 46
  verifying, 46, 58
  weekly, 136
baseline, 42, 76, 118
beep codes, 18
benchmark, 76
BIOS (Basic Input/Output System), 12, 50
  compatibility, 62
  RAID controllers, 58
  revision level, 20, 62
  SCSI controllers, 58
  updating, 62
BIOS utility, 120
boot disks, 22, 34
Boot.ini file, 72
bottlenecks, identifying, 118
brownouts, 12

C

Cables, 6, 10, 72
calls for support during installation
  documentation, 44
Category 5 cables, 10
CD (compact disc), 28
CD-R/CD-RW drives, 134
certificates and security, 44
Cheyenne ArcServe, 136, 138
Chkdisk utility, 98
CMAs (cable management arms), 8, 32
coaxial cables, 6
cold site, 144
COM (communications) port, 6
Compaq Web site, 36
Components, 104
  defective, 102
  ESD, 80
  verifying delivery of, 6
  weight, 8
controllers
  alerts, 18
  master/slave settings, 56
cooling system, 124
Cpucheck command, 94
CPUs
  redundancy, 124
  researching information, 48
  upgrading, 48–53
crimping, 10
critical errors, 106
crossover cables, 10
current backups, 34
customers
  completing steps suggested by previous
    technician, 108
  verifying information, 90
cyber locks, 86

D

daily backups, 136
DAT (Digital Audio Tape), 134
data
  protection, 38
  recovery, 138
  redundancy, 124
  restoration, 138
defective
  components, 102
  FRUs (field replaceable units), 104
  hardware, 102, 144
Dell Web site, 36
devices
  configuring, 32
  device drivers, 18

firmware, 22
  having their own power, 18
  HCLs, 64
  incorrect configuration or upgrade, 120
  not showing up during POST, 18
  polling, 78
  power, 16
  power and voltage regulations and
    availability, 4
  removing, 16
  resource allocation, 16, 18
  resources, 4
  settings, 20
  spare, 126
  threshold level, 78
  warranty information, 4
df command, 96
diagnostic
  hardware and software tools and utilities,
    92–117
  messages, 40
  utilities, 94
diagonal cutters, 10
differential backups, 46, 74, 136
disaster recovery
  backup and recovery schemes, 136–139
  backup hardware, 134
  cold site, 144
  fault-tolerant server environment, 128
  hot fixing, 126
  hot site, 144
  hot spare, 126
  hot swapping, 126
  offsite storage for backups, 138
  redundancy, 124
  warm swap, 126
disaster recovery plan, 130 132, 142, 146
disk arrays, 118
disk controller failures, 128
disk mirroring, 24
disk utilization, 42
Display Processors command, 94
DLT (Digital Linear Tape) drives, 134
DMI (Desktop Management Interface), 114
documentation, 132
  calls for support during installation, 44
  configuration changes for memory, 60
  disaster recovery plan, 142
  equipment sources, 44
  external devices, 4
  hardware, 82
  installation, 44
  location of sources of equipment, 44
  offsite storage, 138
  peripherals, 4, 66
  planning installation, 2
  from previous technicians, 108